D1478639

MAKERS
of the
MUSLIM
WORLD

Mehmed Ali

SELECTION OF TITLES IN THE MAKERS OF THE MUSLIM WORLD SERIES

Series editor: Patricia Crone,
Institute for Advanced Study, Princeton

For current information and details of other books in the
series, please visit www.oneworld-publications.com

MAKERS
of the
MUSLIM
WORLD

Mehmed Ali

From Ottoman Governor to Ruler of Egypt

KHALED FAHMY

ONEWORLD
OXFORD

A Oneworld Book

Published by Oneworld Publications 2009

Copyright © Khaled Fahmy 2009

ISBN 978–1–85168–570–7

Typeset by Jayvee, Trivandrum, India
Printed and bound in India for Imprint Digital

Oneworld Publications
185 Banbury Road
Oxford OX2 7AR
England
www.oneworld-publications.com

Learn more about Oneworld. Join our mailing list to
find out about our latest titles and special offers at:

www.oneworld-publications.com

CONTENTS

ACKNOWLEDGMENTS

When Oneworld Publications first contacted me to write this study of Mehmed Ali Pasha I did not hesitate for long, thinking that this would be an opportunity to go through the notes I had gathered about the man and to piece together the thoughts I had formed about his rule over the past fifteen years. As it turned out, things were not that simple. Mehmed Ali remains a very controversial figure in modern Egyptian and Middle Eastern history, and as I have tried to show in the last chapter this controversy reflects itself not only in his very name and in the evaluation of his legacy, but also in how the original sources, whether archival documents or published books, talked about him. I therefore found myself compelled to conduct further extensive research in the Egyptian National Archives rereading old letters of his and searching for new ones. A sabbatical leave from New York University during 2006 gave me that opportunity. I would like to thank the different archivists and employees there, especially Dr. Mohammad Saber 'Arab, Dr. Abdelwahid Abdelwahid and Ms. Nadia Mostafa, for helping me trace much of the Pasha's correspondence and, in general, for facilitating research in the Archives.

Patricia Crone at Oneworld, the editor of the series in which this book appears, provided invaluable criticism that was frank and constructive. I am grateful to her for showing me that the first draft I presented for the book had missed some crucial points and I thank her and Mike Harpley for their patience while I did the necessary changes and rewrites. A second draft was subjected to equally frank criticism by Roger Owen and Sherif Younis and I thank them for pointing out serious omissions and some very grave discrepancies. I have tried to make the most of their comments but I cannot escape responsibility for the omissions and errors that still remain. My thanks also go to Jaroslaw Dobrowolski for his graciousness in providing the map on pp. viii–ix. Finally, I cannot thank Hossam Bahgat enough for being my most dedicated and most critical reader and for his continuing love, support and inspiration.

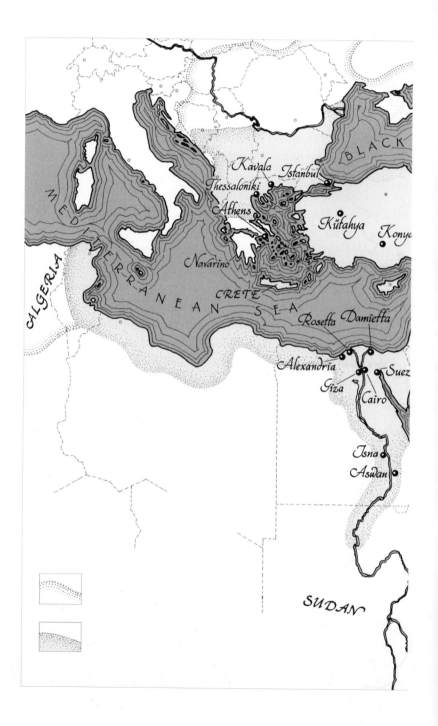

CALGERIA

M E D I T E R R A N E A N   S E A

Kavala   Istanbul

Thessaloniki

Athens

Navarino

CRETE

BLACK

Kütahya   Konya

Rosetta   Damietta

Alexandria   Suez

Giza   Cairo

Isna

Aswan

SUDAN

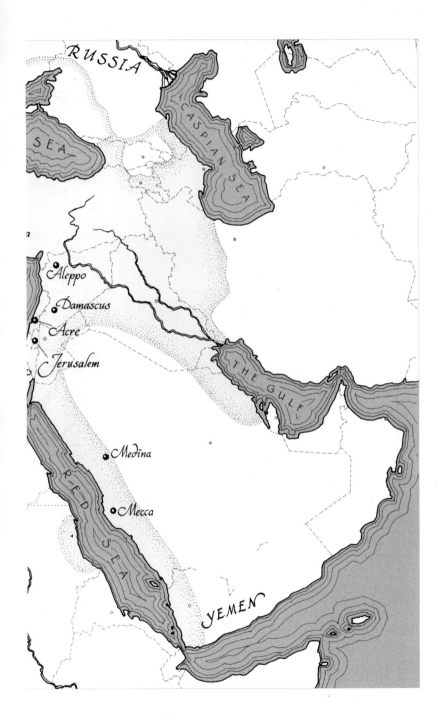

RUSSIA

CASPIAN SEA

SEA

Aleppo

Damascus

Acre

Jerusalem

THE GULF

Medina

RED SEA

Mecca

YEMEN

MACEDONIAN ORIGINS

Approaching Kavala by the highway that links it to Thessaloniki about 130 kilometers further west, one is immediately struck by the serene beauty of this small Greek town. Hugged by lush hills from three sides, the town spreads along the narrow coastal plain and faces south towards the island of Thasos whose Ypsario mountains hover serenely above the blue Aegean haze. The lush mountainous landscape to the north gradually slopes down to tobacco-growing fields and drained marshlands supporting rice cultivation. Bee-keeping hives and vineyards dot the landscape and are evidence of the rich agricultural economy of the town's hinterland.

Placed within a setting of exquisite natural beauty, Kavala's topography also reveals a long and rich history. The Byzantine walls surrounding the old Ottoman town, at the top of which stands an impressive Byzantine castle, are a reminder of the strategic importance the town played for the Byzantine Empire. The famous Via Egnatia linking the ancient city of Rome via the Adriatic through Macedonia and Thrace, to the "new" Rome, i.e. Constantinople, runs literally through the town. Just a few kilometers further north is the famous archaeological site of ancient Philippi, where the fate of the Roman Empire was decided in 42 BCE and where, nearly a century later, St Paul halted to build the first Christian church in Europe. And as if these Roman, Christian and Byzantine pasts are not impressive enough, Kavala also witnessed an important phase of its history when the Ottoman Sultan Murad I incorporated it into his empire in 1387. The long Ottoman era left its mark on the topography of the town, most notably by the impressive aqueduct supplying the city with fresh water, and by the large mosque in the city center – now the Church of St Nicholas – both built by Ibrahim Pasha, grand vizier to Sultan Süleyman the Magnificent.

It was in this town in Rumelia, as the European part of the Ottoman Empire is known, that Mehmed Ali was born in the third quarter of the eighteenth century. How this man crossed the Mediterranean Sea to Egypt, how he established himself as ruler of this important Ottoman province for almost half a century, and how he founded a dynasty there that ruled for a hundred years after his death – all these events add up to a fascinating story. Referred to in Ottoman historiography as Kavalalı Mehmed Ali Paşa and in Egyptian historiography usually under the Arabic spelling of his name, Muhammad 'Ali, he came to be known as the "founder of modern Egypt". Using the name by which he was known in his Turkish mother tongue – Mehmed Ali – he was to become one of the most remarkable men in modern Islamic history and, as we shall see, his life story offers an insight into an intriguing chapter of the history of modern Egypt. Moreover, the policies he pursued as ruler of Egypt constituted one of the most dangerous threats facing the Ottoman Empire during its long history. The following pages tell the story of this remarkable man.

BIRTH

1769 is usually thought to be the year in which Mehmed Ali was born, being the one he chose as his year of birth in the many interviews he would conduct with foreign visitors when he became the ruler of Egypt. This was perhaps to remind his eager listeners that it was also the year in which Napoleon and Wellington were born, two statesmen he admired and with whom he wanted to be associated. Nevertheless, a commemorative medal struck in 1847 at the time of the inauguration of the barrages across the Nile at the apex of the Delta states that Mehmed Ali was born in 1184 AH (or

1770–1771 CE). This, together with information inscribed on his tomb, leads us to believe that the real year of his birth was more likely to have been 1770.

The difficulty in determining Mehmed Ali's birth is but one example of the obscurity which surrounded his life before he left for Egypt in 1801. From humble origins and with no official positions or great deeds attributed to him by then, there are few reasons why Mehmed Ali would have left any significant traces in history books that related to his life in Rumelia. Later, as ruler of Egypt he was amenable to telling stories of his earlier life to interested foreigners keen to record the experiences of someone who they believed was a great oriental ruler; but even so, he was never very forthcoming with details of his youth. He once told a German prince:

> I do not love this period of my life … It is enough if posterity
> knows that all Mehemet Ali has attained he owes neither to birth
> nor [to] interest – to no one but himself. My history, however,
> shall not commence till the period when, free from all restraint, I
> could arouse [Egypt], which I love as my own country, from the
> sleep of ages and mould it to a new existence. (Pückler-Muskau,
> 1845, I, 317–318)

As much as Mehmed Ali would have liked to forget his early years in Kavala – which he came to describe as years of "combat and misery, cunning and bloodshed" – it is impossible to conceal the facts from future generations as he would have wished. Arriving neither as an infant nor even an adolescent, he was already over thirty years old when he landed in Alexandria, by which time he had already married and fathered five children. Even although he lived there for almost fifty years and his fame and glory were tied to Egypt – "my country" as he came to call it – one cannot dismiss the fact that those formative years in Rumelia were bound to have influenced his Egyptian policies and outlook on life in general.

CHILDHOOD AND ADOLESCENCE

Few facts can be established about these early years with any degree of certainty. However, there is no doubt surrounding the identity of his father – a man called Ibrahim Ağa, the son of Osman Ağa, son of Ibrahim Ağa. Family tradition maintained that Ibrahim Ağa was not originally from Kavala and that his paternal grandfather had hailed from Konya in central Anatolia. Before then the family traced its origins to areas further east, which gave rise to an idea that they were originally Kurds. Be that as it may, by the time they settled in Kavala in ca. 1700, they had lost whatever Kurdish identity they might have had; their language was Turkish, they professed Sunni Islam and intermingled with Rumelia's population of Muslims, Jews and Orthodox Christians who were all subjects of the Ottoman sultan.

Beyond his name, little else is known of Mehmed Ali's father. In some accounts he is described as having some military position, most likely as head of night sentries who guarded the highways which led to and from Kavala. His relationship with his son Mehmed Ali appears to have been ambivalent. On the one hand Mehmed Ali recalled with admiration and gratitude that, having survived infancy, he was singled out by his father and brought up in a cushioned atmosphere; but then again, he also appeared resentful of his father precisely for this pampered upbringing. He once recollected that his parents were very protective of him and were eager to "bring me up [as] a gentleman. Hence I soon became effeminate and indolent; my young companions began to despise me and used frequently to cry out, 'what will become of Mehemet Ali, who has nothing and is fit for nothing!'" When he turned fifteen, he added, he became determined to overcome this timidity and to undertake a rigorous regime of physical exercise and self discipline, which included fasting and sleep deprivation for days on end (Pückler-Muskau, 1845, I, 318).

Perhaps it was this ambivalent relationship with his father, together with his desire to emphasize that he was a self-made man, which lay behind Mehmed Ali's later claim that his father had died while he was an infant, and then his mother when he was a small child. This is simply not true, for Ibrahim Ağa's tombstone in Kavala clearly states that he died in 1205 AH/1790–1 CE, i.e. when Mehmed Ali was twenty years old, while his mother's tombstone states that she died five years later in 1210 AH/1795–6 CE, by which time Mehmed Ali had married and already fathered three children.

As for his mother, little is known about her other than her name, Zeyneb Hatun, and that she was from a small village called Nusretli in the province of Drama to the north of Kavala. She too might have been soft with her son and have contributed to what Mehmed Ali later thought was a pampered upbringing. It is very likely that Zeyneb's brother was governor of Kavala ('Arif, n.d., I, fol. 3), which would have enabled her to secure a place for her son in any of the local Quran schools so he could learn how to read and write; in fact, she did nothing of the kind and her son became literate only much later in life when he turned forty. Without literacy, Mehmed Ali would have been unable to secure a position as scribe that his uncle or uncle's friend, the governor of the province of Drama, might have provided him with. He therefore tried his luck in the tobacco trade which his father is recorded as having been engaged in on the side. This brief encounter with trade is what gave rise to the notion that Mehmed Ali was a merchant by profession before he arrived in Egypt. While it is not clear how long he may have helped his father in this business, if at all, he did not need to be personally engaged with trade in order to appreciate fully its importance. Kavala was surrounded by tobacco fields of the finest quality, and the city itself, while lacking a deep natural harbor, was of prime commercial significance because of its strategic location on the road connecting Thessaloniki to Istanbul – two of the largest and busiest commercial centers of the Ottoman Empire.

It is not with his mercantile astuteness that Mehmed Ali tried to impress his foreign admirers in the few reminiscences which are to be found concerning his adolescence. Rather, the emphasis was on his will-power and how he overcame whatever deficiency he thought he had been saddled with; of challenging his playmates to physical exercises; of picking up horsemanship and mastering it; and of

ultimately forcing his friends to recognize him as their peer, even as
having a slight edge over them. Of the many stories that he was fond
of telling, the following extract captures the themes of fortitude,
determination, self discipline and superiority that he wanted to
impress upon his listeners.

> I well recollect our laying a wager one very stormy day, to row over
> to a small island, which still remains in my possession, I was the only
> one who reached it, but although the skin came off my hands, I would
> not suffer the most intense pain to divert me from my purpose. In this
> manner I continued to invigorate both mind and body, till, as I have
> already told you, I afterwards found ample opportunity in a graver
> sphere of action, to prove my courage to myself and others during
> petty warfare in our villages. (Pückler-Muskau, 1845, I, 318)

Here, as in many other stories, a picture emerges of a young lad
who is far from being timid or soft. Gone were the days when he felt
intimidated by his playmates; if anything, it was now he who was
intimidating them. In fact, from these stories one can discern the
coming of age of a man who could see through his playmates' souls
and who had managed to mould them into a group of dedicated and
admiring followers. His remarkable leadership qualities could be discerned from these early days by his ability to inspire admiration in
some of the young men who gathered around him, while coaxing, if
not bullying, others into doing his bidding. And it is not difficult to
see from these stories that some of his fellow inhabitants, as well as
the residents of nearby towns, were aware of a reputation he was
building as someone who could set things right and address local
grievances in a swift and decisive manner.

In one story, for example, we are told that Mehmed Ali went to his
uncle, the governor of Kavala, and offered to help him deal with
some recalcitrant villages who refused to pay their taxes. After some
hesitation, the governor gave him the go-ahead, and immediately the
young lad set out with his followers to one of these villages. Rather
than confront its able-bodied men on their own territory, he

proceeded to the village mosque as if to pray. Secretly, though, he had sent some of his men to summon four senior villagers to meet him in the mosque. The unsuspecting men obliged, only to realize that they had been arrested and taken hostage. Eventually, the entire village grudgingly agreed to pay back its tax arrears.

MARRIAGE

While the governor must have been pleased that the taxes were collected, he was not particularly thrilled by the manner in which his nephew had managed to do so. He believed that something needed to be done to calm the lad down, and so he was probably extremely relieved when he heard from his nephew that he was thinking to marry and start a family. On one of his trips to nearby Drama to visit the governor of that town Mehmed Ali had asked if there was a suitable young girl to whom he could get married. He was told that there was indeed a young woman called Emine from the village of Nusretli, the same village from which his mother had come; in fact, he might even have heard of this young woman, for she had become the talk of town after her previous husband had been shot dead before the marriage was consummated, leaving her a small fortune. Given the difference in social standing between himself and Emine, Mehmed Ali did not take the governor's proposal very seriously. However, much to his pleasant surprise, he discovered that the governor was indeed serious about his offer and that his uncle was pushing for it. Since it was understood that Mehmed Ali would move to Nusretli and set up home in his new wife's house there, what better way, his uncle must have thought, to help the young lad to settle down?

Mehmed Ali's marriage to Emine took place in 1787, when he was seventeen years old, and she was to remain his devoted wife for the next thirty-seven years until she died in Alexandria in 1823. Together they had five children, all born in Nusretli while the family still lived there: Tevhide (1787–1830), Ibrahim (1789–1848), Ahmed Tousson (1793–1816), Ismail (1795–1822) and Nazlı (a.k.a. Hatice,

1799–1860). (After Emine's death Mehmed Ali had many other wives and concubines with whom he had probably about twenty children, most of whom died in infancy.)

The young Mehmed Ali supported his growing family by investing his wife's small wealth in the lucrative tobacco trade. It seems though that Mehmed Ali's old friends did not leave him alone and every now and then they would call on him to accompany them on one of their little escapades. It was one of these outings that proved to be one misadventure too many for his uncle, prompting him to think that he needed to think of somewhere further afield to which he could send his nephew.

The incident involved a man by the name of Ağu who, like Mehmed Ali, was from Kavala and who was also reputed to be brave and strong. This Ağu fell out with his own brother, Osman Ağa, who eventually killed him and sought refuge in the house of Mehmed Ali's uncle, the governor of Kavala. Without seeking his uncle's permission, Mehmed Ali and his small gang stormed into the governor's house, seized the killer, dragged him out of the house and hanged him on a nearby tree. The governor was enraged that his nephew had taken the law into his own hands; but at the same time there was little he could do, given the young man's growing popularity and his ability to set things right.

Eventually he found an ingenious way out. Three years earlier, the entire Ottoman world had been shocked by news from Egypt that a large French army had landed there headed by a general known as Bonaparte who, young though he was, had already made a name for himself in Italy. This news came as a complete surprise, given that France was a traditional European ally of the Ottoman Empire. As part of his empire since 1517, the sultan could not afford to lose such a pivotal province as Egypt, the governor of which contributed a sizeable annual tribute. In addition, he was entrusted with the important duty of protecting the pilgrimage routes to Mecca and Medina. By the time diplomatic negotiations failed in 1801, the sultan was determined to evict the French by force, having received firm assurances from the British that they would assist him in his endeavor. An army of newly trained troops was dispatched by land via Syria led by the grand vizier, Yusuf Ziya Pasha. The sultan hoped to raise a further force of 4000 troops in Rumelia, and orders were sent to the governor of Kavala to collect 300 irregular troops for dispatch to Egypt.

This, then, was the governor's opportunity to be free of his troublesome nephew. He approached the governor of Rumelia with boastful claims about Mehmed Ali's valor and bravery and managed to enlist his nephew in the troops destined for Egypt. In fact Mehmed Ali was appointed as second in command of that force, which was to be led by the governor's own son, Ali Ağa. Leaving behind his wife and children, Mehmed Ali thus embarked on a trip that was to change the course of his life, as well as the fate of Egypt and of the Ottoman world.

2

THE EGYPTIAN QUAGMIRE

By the time Mehmed Ali arrived in Egypt in 1801 the country had been ravaged by incessant warfare against *l'Armé de l'Orient*, the French army of occupation. For three years the French struggled to pacify the country and to establish a foothold in the eastern Mediterranean. The young general, Napoleon Bonaparte, had hoped this would be a springboard to spread French influence further east in order to threaten British possessions in India. However, the Egyptian population – whether in the cities or in the countryside, and as much in the Delta as in Upper Egypt – was not easily persuaded by Bonaparte's proclamation that he had nothing but respect for Islam, and that the French had arrived only to get rid of the local warlords, the Mamluks, and to return Egypt to the Ottoman fold. Armed resistance was mounted by Bedouins in the desert, by peasants in the countryside and by the urban population. Cairo rose not once but twice and the French suppressed these two uprisings in a very brutal fashion.

The most serious military opposition, however, was mounted from the south by the Mamluks. For centuries these warlords had established military households where they trained boys and young men who had been captured or bought from Caucasia and Georgia to be their pages, bodyguards, servants and military retainers; the Arabic word *mamluk* means "taken into possession". By the time Bonaparte's troops invaded Egypt, the Mamluks had entrenched themselves firmly in the country and each Mamluk grandee (*bey*) had established a household (*bayt*) that was composed of privy chambers,

gardens, kitchens, segregated women's quarters and, most significantly, barracks. By engaging in lucrative trade (especially in Yemeni
coffee) and by using their military force to collect taxes from the
countryside, the Mamluk grandees replenished their coffers and
were thus able to recruit more young men from Georgia. They also
managed to send on to Istanbul some of the taxes they had collected,
thus achieving a precarious *modus vivendi* with the capital of the
Ottoman Empire.

Bonaparte's invasion seriously challenged this effective control
that the Mamluk beys had established within Egypt. The French
drove them from their mansions in Cairo, cut off their trade routes
with Arabia and Yemen, and confiscated their agricultural fiefs.
After being defeated in the Battle of the Pyramids (21 July 1798), the
Mamluks retreated to the south from where they continued to attack
French troops. One of their leaders, Ibrahim Bey, sought refuge in
Syria and launched attacks on the French from there.

It was this complex military situation that Mehmed Ali found in
Egypt when he arrived there in the spring of 1801. Aged thirty-one
and at the height of his physical prowess, and with some combat
experience already under his belt, the military situation he now confronted was considerably more complex than anything he had experienced in Kavala and Nusretli. Moreover, the leader of the small
Kavalian contingent, Ali Ağa – the son of the governor who had been
his friend and ally – for some mysterious reason midway through the
trip to Egypt decided to return home, leaving Mehmed Ali in charge
of this small troop of men. To compound matters, this force was soon
joined by a much larger one, reported to be around 4000 strong,
composed of Albanian irregulars who were famous throughout the
Ottoman Empire for their unruly, impetuous behavior – but who
were equally known for their zeal and bravery. Speaking a different
tongue and coming from the other side of the Balkans, these soldiers
would be much more difficult to harness than the fellow Kavalians
Mehmed Ali currently had under his command. (As will be seen
later, Mehmed Ali's close association with the Albanians gave rise to
the erroneous idea that he was an ethnic Albanian.)

To further complicate what was already a complex situation, the naval force that he found himself a part of was headed by none other than Hüseyin Pasha, the grand admiral of the Ottoman navy. Before setting off for Egypt the grand admiral had overseen the training of troops intended to form the nucleus of a new standing army, an army which the sultan hoped would enable his admiral to assert control over the provinces of his far-flung empire. The grand admiral had with him some 1200 of these men in the hope that he could test them in Egypt to prove that they were worth the financial and political gamble incurred in training them. Known as the *nizam-i cedid*, or New Order, these troops would eventually play a decisive role in the history of the empire.

Finally, and adding to the already confusing military situation, Mehmed Ali soon discovered that he and this motley group of Ottoman troops were to be joined by the British fleet who were intent on evicting the French from Egypt. Right from the start of Bonaparte's campaign the British had quite rightly seen the French attack on Egypt as a threat to their Indian possessions and were keen to thwart the French attempt to establish a foothold in Egypt. Rear admiral Horatio Nelson had already succeeded in destroying the French fleet at the so-called Battle of the Nile (1–2 August 1798), and three years later the British were only too eager to answer the sultan's plea for help in evicting the French army from Egypt. In short, confronted with the then leading military powers of the world, as well as Hüseyin Pasha with his specially trained *nizam-i cedid* troops, what Mehmed Ali came face to face with was the most daring and original attempt at military reform within the Ottoman Empire to date.

HÜSREV PASHA: THE BEGINNING OF A LIFELONG ENMITY

After weeks at sea the Egyptian shores finally appeared on the horizon and, within a short time of his debarkation, Mehmed Ali found himself engaged in a minor military attack on a French post. In charge of this attack was the grand admiral's lieutenant, Mehmed Hüsrev Pasha, who was to become Mehmed Ali's lifelong nemesis. Their conflicting paths were to cross numerous times over the next fifty years.

Hüsrev was some ten years Mehmed Ali's senior and the two men had radically different backgrounds. Unlike Mehmed Ali, Hüsrev came from the very center of the Ottoman Empire and was educated in the imperial palace. As a young Georgian slave who had been bought by Hüseyin Pasha, Hüsrev was raised in his master's own household where the grand admiral nurtured him and accepted him as one of his closest protégés. Hüsrev eventually married two women from the imperial household, both freed-women; the first had been owned by the sultan's mother, and the second by the sultan's sister who also happened to be the grand admiral's wife.

Accompanied by the Albanian and Kavalian troops and the large Ottoman army, both officers marched with all their men south to Cairo after what had been their first military action in Egypt. There they were met with another section of the Ottoman army, headed by the grand vizier, Yusuf Ziya Pasha. The combined Ottoman forces of land and naval troops then entered Cairo in July 1801 and were warmly received by the city's jubilant crowds who cheered as the soldiers marched through the markets shouting, "May God make the sultan victorious" (Jabarti, 1994, III, 389).

After reaching an agreement with the French stipulating their withdrawal, Hüseyin Pasha departed from Cairo heading north to board his ships. The French army soon evacuated Egypt, bringing an end to an occupation that had lasted a little over three years. In a clear sign that the Ottomans were intent on returning Egypt to their fold they appointed a new governor to rule Egypt in the sultan's name. This was none other than Hüseyin Pasha's protégé, Hüsrev Pasha.

Things did not return to normal, for although Istanbul's authority was now officially restored the question of the Mamluk beys who had implicitly challenged that authority was not yet resolved. The

Mamluk fighting power had certainly been weakened after three years of incessant fighting against the French. In fact, never having been a single entity, the Mamluks were now even more divided than ever before. This was further compounded by the death from plague of one of their leaders, Murad Bey, in the spring of 1801 and the departure of his rival, Ibrahim Bey, to Syria during the French occupation. The leadership of the Mamluk factions therefore went to two beys from Murad Bey's household, 'Uthman Bey al-Bardisi and Muhammad Bey al-Alfi.

Capitalizing on this division, the Ottoman authorities in Egypt – namely the grand vizier and the grand admiral – attempted to end Mamluk presence there once and for all. It was suspected that the Mamluk beys were secretly negotiating with the British; on 20 October 1801, the grand vizier invited them to Cairo and immediately put nine of them under arrest. Two days later the grand admiral invited the Mamluk beys who were in Alexandria to his flagship. Not aware of what had happened to their brethren in Cairo, they responded to the grand admiral's invitation, only to be confronted with what they were told were the sultan's conditions for an amnesty on their past deeds: an oath of allegiance to be sworn to the sultan and an agreement to accompany the grand admiral to Istanbul. In spite of some glitches in execution, the plot seems to have succeeded; the Mamluk beys found themselves trapped and those who had not accepted the invitations, most notably al-Alfi Bey, were chased south by Tahir Pasha, the commander of the Albanian soldiers. However, just before they were to be shipped to the Ottoman capital – where the Mamluk beys feared a grim fate awaited them – word reached the British of what had befallen their Mamluk allies. This prompted them to protest strongly to the Ottomans and they eventually managed to free the Mamluk beys.

This incident illustrates the precarious balance of power in Egypt subsequent to the French withdrawal. The Ottoman sultan, legally the rightful sovereign of the country, could not effectively establish his control there, even with the presence of his grand vizier and his grand admiral. The Mamluk beys on the other hand were divided and weak and managed to escape from the sultan's wrath only by the skin of their teeth – and only with British assistance. On their part, although the British were eager to assist their Mamluk allies and to reinstate them in their former estates in Egypt, they insisted that this be conditional on their acknowledgement of the sultan's suzerainty. In other words, the British had to balance their desire to assist their allies in Egypt with the dangers of jeopardizing the sultan's authority and the threat of destabilization to his empire.

Not surprisingly, six months after Mehmed Ali had landed in Egypt the political situation was still very volatile even if militarily the dangers were less acute. A cessation of hostilities was officially declared when a peace treaty between the French and the Ottomans was signed on 9 October 1801, and the British eventually withdrew all their forces from Egypt in March 1803 after supervising the French evacuation. This was followed by the departure of the Ottoman military forces which included both the New Order troops that had arrived with the grand admiral, and the Janissary land army that the grand vizier had arrived with; these armies left respectively from Alexandria on 21 November 1801, and via Syria on 13 February 1802.

Even although the Ottomans had withdrawn their forces from Egypt, they were in fact keen to re-establish their hegemony over this important province. They entrusted their new governor, Hüsrev Pasha, to fight the Mamluk beys mercilessly, while reasserting Istanbul's control over Egypt. The Mamluks however proved much harder to subdue than Istanbul had imagined. For one thing, at the same time as demanding rewards for fighting the French, the Mamluk leaders were also keen to repossess the properties that the French had confiscated from them; for another, Hüsrev lacked the military means necessary to subdue them, let alone deal them a death blow.

What Hüsrev had under his command was a small garrison of Janissary troops. With the Mamluks controlling much of Upper Egypt and gradually re-establishing their control over the rich lands of the Delta, Hüsrev was unable to raise the taxes required to pay the soldiers under his command, let alone raise new troops. He therefore relied on the only significant force in Egypt at the time, namely, the 4000-strong Albanian contingent under the command of Tahir Pasha and his deputy Mehmed Ali who in late 1801 had been promoted to the rank of *sarcheshme*, or quartermaster. Assisted by both Tahir and Mehmed Ali, Hüsrev launched one attack after another against the Mamluks in the Delta, but they all failed to inflict a decisive defeat on them. This prompted Istanbul to send Hüsrev a harsh official rebuke.

In an attempt to implement these instructions, Hüsrev set about preparing for another major offensive against the Mamluks. Without access to horses, he issued orders to the Cairo donkey-drivers to gather as many donkeys as they could find in the city; in total some 3000 donkeys were brought together which prompted the populace to refer sarcastically to the Pasha's much hoped for expedition as the "Expedition of the Donkeys". When Hüsrev finally confronted his adversaries near Damanhour in the middle of the Delta, the Mamluks, who were known to be superb cavalrymen, inflicted a heavy defeat on him. Significantly, during battle Mehmed Ali stood by and refused to engage with the enemy or to assist Hüsrev. What is more, after the battle he sent his Albanian troops to Cairo to ask for their pay. Hüsrev could not believe his ears. "By what right do you deserve to be paid when you have accomplished nothing?" he asked them. He then summoned Mehmed Ali to the Citadel in the middle of the night to interrogate him about his questionable conduct during and after the battle. Mehmed Ali, in a clear act of defiance, refused to go and cited some vague pretext. Jabarti comments on this tension between both men by saying,

> This fiasco [the defeat of Damanhour] caused an estrangement
> between the pasha and the army ... Mehmed Ali Sarcheshme was the
> most prominent man among them. The pasha tried to trap him [by
> inviting him to the Citadel], but with no success, for he was
> extremely cautious ... This was the first appearance of Mehmed Ali,
> and from this time forward his importance increased. (Jabarti,
> 1994, IV, 46)

During his early days as governor of Egypt Hüsrev had managed to restore some tranquility to the Cairo markets and people sensed that it would be he who would impose peace after years of occupation, war and famines. However, any attempt to spread his influence beyond Cairo required Hüsrev to raise new troops which begged the question of how they would be paid. At a certain point Hüsrev set about training some of his slaves along French lines, but this too raised speculation about how he would meet the cost of their uniforms and their food. Running out of options, the governor was forced to impose a three-year poll-tax on the Cairo population without having a reliable military force to gather it.

To make matters worse, the Albanian troops headed by Tahir Pasha and Mehmed Ali broke out into an open mutiny on 29 April 1803. As had happened before, the troops were asking for their back-pay. When Hüsrev told them that the coffers were empty the troops ran amok in the city. The markets were closed and people hid in their own homes, but, even so, much looting and killing went on and the city rapidly spiraled out of control. After four days of intense fighting, Hüsrev's own house was attacked and soon razed to the ground. Conscious that he had no future in Cairo, Hüsrev fled the city with his harem and headed to Damietta guarded by a small contingent of supporters, with the Albanian troops close at his heels (Jabarti, 1994, III, 364–372).

This was to be the first of many rounds of confrontation between Mehmed Ali and Hüsrev, and although Jabarti, our main source of information about these bloody events, does not point the finger at Mehmed Ali directly, it is not difficult to see his hand in what had taken place. He might not have been the main instigator of the mutiny but as second in command of the Albanian troops he could have found ways to pacify them if he had so wished. However, given that his immediate commander, Tahir Pasha, was laying the blame on Hüsrev, and encouraging his soldiers to demand their arrears from him, Mehmed Ali apparently decided to go with the flow in spite of the enormous risks involved in doing nothing to quell a rebellion against the representative of the sultan.

Now that Cairo's legitimate ruler had been deposed the situation in the city had become even more precarious, and with all these troops (Albanians, Janissaries, Bedouins) running amok in the streets demanding their arrears when the treasury had literally been depleted, more trouble was certain to come. This time it was the Janissary troops who, besides demanding their pay, were anxious about the growing power of the Albanians and how they "looked down on [the Janissaries] and regarded them with contempt, in spite of the fact that the Janissaries held a high opinion of themselves and looked on themselves as the mainstay of the empire, viewing the Albanians as their servants, their soldiers and their subordinates" (Jabarti, 1994, III, 376). Almost a month after the outbreak of the unrest, on 26 May rumors started to circulate that Tahir was about to reach an accommodation with the Mamluks, which prompted the Janissaries to go to ask him for their pay. In the past Tahir had used Hüsrev as a pretext and urged the Janissaries to go to him, while making sure that his own Albanian troops were paid. This time, however, with Hüsrev out of the picture, Tahir failed to shrug off the Janissaries and, after a heated argument with around 250 of them in his own house, one of the soldiers drew his sword and chopped off his head tossing it through the window and into the courtyard below. A bloodbath then ensued between the Janissaries and the Albanians on the streets of Cairo and there appeared to be no force powerful enough to stop the competing troops from sacking the city.

After Tahir's assassination the leadership of the Albanian contingent passed to Mehmed Ali and he thus became commander of a significant military force that was second only to that of the Mamluks. During the two years since his arrival in Egypt with the Albanians he had managed to cultivate good relations with their leaders with the result that he was often considered as an Albanian himself. He could now count on their loyalty, something that Hüsrev never could. Furthermore, with the legitimate representative of Istanbul under siege in Damietta, Mehmed Ali was in an unrivaled position of power.

At this moment, however, Mehmed Ali's status was threatened by an unlikely character, and the manner in which he dealt with this unexpected threat gives us one of the earliest indications that he had a clear sense of his role in the rapidly evolving situation. Two months earlier in March 1803 a certain Ahmed Pasha, who had been appointed by Istanbul as governor of Medina in Arabia, stopped in Egypt on his way to his new post. On the same day that Tahir was assassinated Ahmed Pasha attempted to fill the power vacuum by convening the shaykhs of the centuries-old mosque-university of al-Azhar and briefed them as to what had happened. He then dispatched them to Mehmed Ali demanding his submission, the implication being that this would result in his departure from Egypt and his repatriation. Mehmed Ali's response was as significant as it was swift. As soon as he heard what the shaykhs had to say, he declared that Ahmed Pasha had no authority in Egypt, given that he had been appointed as governor of Medina and had no connection to Egypt. He added, "I was the one who appointed Tahir Pasha to be guardian of the Egyptian domain on behalf of the empire, he [i.e. Tahir] had some sort of connection (with Egypt). Ahmed Pasha, however, has none whatsoever. He is leaving the country and taking the Janissaries with him. We are fitting him out and he is going off to his province [that he had been appointed to]" (Jabarti, 1994, III, 378).

Besides the fact that this is the earliest recorded statement by Mehmed Ali, the significance of these words lies in what they reveal of his way of thinking. Having challenged Ahmed Pasha's authority by arguing that he had no mandate to speak about Egyptian matters, he then asserted his own authority by saying that it was *he* who had appointed Tahir Pasha in the first place – a claim that was not strictly correct. He then carried out *his* own order to Ahmed Pasha at which point a group of Albanian soldiers together with a small Mamluk force chased Ahmed Pasha and his Janissary troops and had them locked up in a mosque just outside the city gates. Significantly, however, in addition to implicitly arguing that his authority derived from the sword, Mehmed Ali reminded the shaykhs of the overall sovereignty of the Ottoman sultan and that even if he, Mehmed Ali, had been instrumental in installing Tahir, he did this "on behalf of the empire". This oscillation between his own self-confidence on the one hand, and the legitimacy that he believed could only be derived from Istanbul on the other, would prove to be a long-lasting feature of Mehmed Ali's mindset and it would continue to dictate his thought and action throughout his life.

Due to the loyalty and assistance of his Albanian troops, Mehmed Ali had managed to strengthen his position in Egypt: he used them to chase Hüsrev out of Cairo; he assumed the leadership of their contingent following Tahir's death; and he succeeded in challenging Ahmed Pasha and removing him from the scene. Even although his position was getting stronger day after day because of his close collaboration with the Albanians, it was equally important for him to secure an alliance with the Mamluks against the Ottoman governor. To achieve this he led a joint expedition with 'Uthman Bey al-Bardisi against Hüsrev in Damietta. After putting up a fierce fight, Hüsrev was taken into custody by them and in July 1803 he re-entered Cairo, this time as a prisoner, with the result that he was unceremoniously locked up in the Citadel.

In the same month Istanbul sent yet another governor, Trabulsi Ali Pasha, to replace Hüsrev Pasha. His orders were to send the Albanian troops to Arabia to fight the Wahhabi rebels who had defied the Sultan's authority there (which we shall return to later). He was also determined to fight the Mamluks and to expel them from Cairo, if not from Egypt altogether. "The sword of the sultanate is long," he warned them. "It may be that the Sultan will seek against you the aid of some of your opponents over whom you have no control." Sensing that the new governor was heading for a bloody confrontation with the Mamluks, Mehmed Ali stepped back, apparently preferring to wait for the outcome. Without enough troops at his disposal Ali Pasha found himself besieged in Alexandria so he hesitated before leaving for Cairo to assume the official reins of power in the Citadel. When he finally dared to march towards the capital he was betrayed by his own guards and slain in the desert.

With this grim fate which befell Istanbul's representative it was becoming increasingly clear that Mehmed Ali and his Albanian forces had become the only significant forces in Egypt. Given that both the

Ottomans and the Mamluks could not settle their scores except through him, this meant that Mehmed Ali effectively held the province in his own hands and that he could end up controlling it alone. But, for this to happen, he could not rely on either of these forces – the Mamluks or the Ottomans – as neither of them would willingly acquiesce to hand him the reins of power to rule alone. To guarantee success, he had to find a third power through which he could assert his own hegemony. This he found in the people of Cairo, both the populace and their leaders – the religious scholars of the venerated al-Azhar Mosque and leading merchants. What proved to be one of his many masterstrokes was his ability to charm the Cairene population sufficiently that they would allow him to carve out a place for himself, and then to impose his will on both the Mamluks and the Ottomans.

THE EVICTION OF THE MAMLUKS FROM CAIRO

Through his careful dealings with the Mamluks Mehmed Ali had succeeded in driving a wedge between their two main leaders, al-Alfi and al-Bardisi. With Bardisi's troops in Cairo at a time when Alfi's soldiers were scattered throughout the provinces, Mehmed Ali decided to seize the initiative. He ordered his Albanian soldiers onto the streets of Cairo and incited them to ask for their arrears. Without an Ottoman governor in the Citadel, Bardisi was forced to deal with the crisis by levying yet another tax on the merchants of Cairo. When this proved to be inadequate to meet the demands of the soldiers, Bardisi went one step further and levied a general tax on all residents of Cairo, based on the value of urban property. News of this tax spread like wildfire from one neighborhood to the next and on 7 March 1804 the masses took to the streets in a huge demonstration carrying banners, dying their hands with indigo, hitting on drums, and shouting, "Of how much will you fleece me, Bardisi?"

The scale of the revolt was unprecedented and caught Bardisi by surprise. Apparently fearing that the people might conclude that these taxes had been imposed by Bardisi in order to pay Mehmed Ali's Albanian soldiers, Mehmed Ali ordered his men to march with the demonstrators and to placate them by saying, "We are with you entirely; you are subjects and we are soldiers. We did not approve of this *firda* [tax]. Our provisions are to be taken from the *miri* [government], not from you. You are poor people" (Jabarti, 1994, III, 435). Mehmed Ali also ordered his deputy to appear among the people to convince them that it was Bardisi and not Mehmed Ali who was behind this detestable tax which had brought them onto the streets in their masses.

With Bardisi on the defensive Mehmed Ali sprinted into action and immediately ordered his troops to attack the houses of all Mamluk beys who were in Cairo at that time, starting with the house of his "friend" Bardisi. With little alternative Bardisi fled the city altogether and was soon followed by all the other Mamluk beys.

SENDING HÜSREV PACKING

Having succeeded in dislodging the Mamluks from Cairo by allying himself with the populace, Mehmed Ali had one last serious hurdle to overcome if he were to establish himself as sole *hegemon*, namely, the Ottoman representative. When he mounted the hill to the Citadel after the departure of the Mamluk troops, Mehmed Ali allowed Hüsrev Pasha his freedom after his eight-month-long imprisonment since July 1803. He then had heralds go through the streets proclaiming an amnesty for all the soldiers engaged in looting and pillage which was declared in the names of both Mehmed Hüsrev Pasha and Mehmed Ali. On hearing his own name Hüsrev was fooled into thinking that he was being restored to his former position, so much so that when he passed by his former, now ruined house on his way down from the Citadel, he issued orders for workers and engineers to rebuild it. It soon became clear to him – and neither was it for the first or the last time – that he had underestimated what Mehmed Ali was capable of, for, rather than finding himself back home and at ease in his restored house, instead he found himself on a boat leaving for Istanbul.

Since Mehmed Ali's arrival in Egypt three years earlier, this period was now the most opportune time for him. He had succeeded in bringing Cairo under his control, given that both the Mamluks and the representative of Ottoman authority were no longer present in the city. Moreover, he had clearly gained the confidence of the city's inhabitants. Above all, he could still count on the loyalty of the Albanian troops who had proved themselves to be the most significant fighting force in the country. However, the big question was – what would Istanbul's next move be?

Before going up to the Citadel to free Hüsrev and to send him packing, Mehmed Ali had received news that a *firman* (an order by the sultan) had arrived which appointed Hurşid Pasha, the previous governor of Alexandria, as the new governor of Egypt; Mehmed Ali was to be relieved of his duties in Egypt and installed as governor of Jidda in Arabia. However, with the capital and its Citadel now under his firm control, Mehmed Ali was in a strong position to frustrate Hurşid's bid for power, especially given that Hurşid had no troops with him in Alexandria. Nevertheless, openly defying Istanbul carried with it the enormous risks of being declared a rebel, and the main element that dictated his tactics vis-à-vis Hurşid was how to balance his confidence in his own strength with the constant need to appease Istanbul.

Everything was now dependent on how Hurşid Pasha would behave. Given his previous tenure as governor of Alexandria he was of course somewhat familiar with Egyptian politics, and bearing the official *firman* of investiture from Istanbul he was not arriving as an insignificant foe in spite of his lack of military support. At the same time, now that the Mamluks had left Cairo Mehmed Ali could no longer use them as a pretext to prevent the new governor from entering the city, nor was it wise to obstruct him by force as this carried with it the odium of being declared a rebel by Istanbul. Mehmed Ali's tactic was to rely on his rising popularity and to control the population's acceptance of Hurşid – made easier when the new governor called for troop reinforcements from Syria, thus making further tax levies inevitable. When some 5000 troops arrived from Syria they indeed proved to be a burden as Hurşid now had to raise a new tax on artisans and merchants to pay for them. This prompted the closure of the markets and ushered in a multi-factional coalition that was to play a decisive role in the confrontation between the two men. This coalition was composed of various elements: leading merchants whose businesses were severely hit by the lack of law and order; the *ulama* (religious scholars) who had been mediating the relationship between rulers and the ruled since the late eighteenth century (first Mamluks, then the French, then Ottoman governors); and the notables whose leader, 'Umar Makram, had appeared during the French occupation as a popular figure capable of mobilizing many segments of the city's population.

Tensions were rising both in the city and in the country at large with the Mamluk forces roaming Upper Egypt and other troops ravaging the Delta. The final showdown came at the beginning of May 1805 when the troops that had arrived from Syria attacked private dwellings in Old Cairo and evicted their residents. This was the straw that broke the camel's back, for when this news spread, Cairo rose up in a huge revolt: shops were closed, people armed themselves and the *ulama* of al-Azhar suspended their lessons and closed down the venerated mosque.

On 12 May 1805 the *ulama* finally decided to act: they gathered at the Cairo Court and drew up a list of demands to pass on to Hurşid. These included their desire that no taxes be levied except with the prior approval of the notables and the *ulama*, as well as their wish that all armed soldiers be barred from entering the city. It was clear from these demands that the *ulama* and the Cairo population as a whole were tired of the pillaging and looting that the soldiers had been engaged in for years. They were also expressing their frustration at the frequency with which the authorities were turning to them, via the imposed taxes, to feed and pay these troops. The *ulama* then delivered these demands to Hurşid who lost no time in dismissing them. The following day on 13 May the *ulama* reconvened and with thousands of restless people gathering outside the court they decided to depose Hurşid and appoint Mehmed Ali instead. They immediately rushed to Mehmed Ali's residence to inform him of their decisions. Appearing calm and serene, Mehmed Ali started by asking the delegation what they had decided upon. "To depose Hurşid," they answered. "And who have you chosen to replace him?" he asked, apparently pretending not to know their answer. "We will accept only you. You will be governor over us according to our conditions, for we know you as a just and good man." Knowing that the *ulama* had no alternative except himself to defuse the crisis, Mehmed Ali initially turned down the offer; but it did not take his guests much effort to persuade him to reconsider.

When Mehmed Ali "reluctantly" agreed to be governor, the delegation then went up to Hurşid in the Citadel to inform him of their decision. Predictably, Hurşid refused to budge and retorted, "I was appointed by the Sultan and will not be removed at the command of the peasants. I will leave the Citadel only on the orders of the imperial government" (Jabarti, 1994, III, 506). A long and bloody standoff ensued with Hurşid fortifying himself in the Citadel and the Albanian troops, together with the people of Cairo led by the *ulama*, most notably 'Umar Makram, fighting Hurşid's troops in the streets. Barricades were put up, cannons were fired from the Citadel onto the city down below, and fierce battles were conducted sometimes from street to street.

The standoff continued for eight weeks and was not broken until 9 July when it was reported that a messenger had arrived with a new *firman* from Istanbul. Neighborhood leaders, senior Albanian officers, turbaned shaykhs, residents of various quarters, and leading merchants all marched behind the courier with drums and wind instruments. Finally the huge crowd stopped at Mehmed Ali's residence, where they were received by him. Once the shaykhs and notables had arrived, the content of the *firman* was read aloud:

> To Mehmed Ali Pasha, former governor of Jidda and present
> governor of Egypt, since 20th of Rabi' I [18 June 1805] when the

ulama and subjects approved of that and of the deposing of Ahmed Pasha [Hurşid] from [the governorship] of Egypt. The latter is to go to Alexandria with all due respect and honor [and wait there] until he receives orders to go to another province (Jabarti, 1994, III, 515).

As soon as Hurşid was informed of the contents of the *firman*, he agreed to end the standoff and descended from the Citadel with his tail between his legs. He was escorted to Alexandria and departed from Egypt on 5 August 1805, never to return. Mehmed Ali was now sole legitimate governor of Egypt.

3

CONSOLIDATION OF POWER

In 1805 at the age of thirty-five, Mehmed Ali found himself legitimate governor of one of the wealthiest provinces of the Ottoman Empire. Four years earlier he had arrived in Egypt as a complete stranger and, speaking only a dialect of Turkish and a sprinkling of Arabic, he virtually had no spoken or written knowledge of the language of this country's majority population; added to which he had neither patron nor even a faint acquaintance in the imperial capital to help nurture and promote his career. Moreover, he had arrived in a land that had been exhausted by three years of French occupation, that had been ravaged by incessant fighting between different warring factions: French, British, Mamluks, Bedouin, Janissaries and Albanians. Nevertheless, in a matter of only four years he found himself in an enviable position. In this short time he was witness to the withdrawal of the French and then the British troops; he had survived the assassination of his friend and ally, Tahir Pasha; and he had seen three successive Ottoman governors come and go, each in turn failing to implement Istanbul's writ in this important province. Concurrent with these events his own position in this new land had grown from strength to strength. He had won the loyalty of the Albanian contingent, the trust of the *ulama* and merchants of Cairo, the allegiance of the city's populace, and – most crucially – Istanbul's approval, albeit reluctant, for him to be its legitimate representative in Egypt.

What is most impressive about these early years in Mehmed Ali's career in Egypt is the dramatic transformation in his character.

During the constant internecine conflicts that Egypt witnessed after the departure of the French, Mehmed Ali no longer presented himself as the impetuous, hot-blooded young man we saw in Kavala and its environs, who often took the law into his own hands. Rather, he presented himself to the warring factions as an outsider with no personal interest – one who could settle disputes and set things right. It was in this capacity as an arbiter that the people of Cairo, the *ulama*, the merchants and notables all turned to him to resolve their deep-seated conflicts and to diffuse the long-standing political stalemate. It is as if he reinvented himself: having decided to cast off the image he had acquired as a village bully, he adopted the role of a true statesman, one who could win the confidence of his allies, inspire respect in his enemies, and expect obedience from his followers.

After receiving the *firman* of investiture on 9 July 1805 Mehmed Ali's position became at a stroke significantly stronger. Although he had already been chosen by the people of Cairo to replace Hurşid, no degree of popular support could match the legitimacy embedded in a sultanic *firman*. Given that he was neither a *sharif* who could claim descent from the Prophet, nor was he a *ghazi* who could argue that he had won Egypt by the sword, but that he was of humble origins without any significant financial resources, and that, above all, he was a stranger to Egypt – and an illiterate one at that – Mehmed Ali's sole source of legitimacy as governor of Egypt was the *firman* that arrived from Istanbul bestowing on him this coveted governorship. However, as we have seen above, the sultan only issued this *firman* with reluctance after his previous attempts to assign other governors had failed. Unlike previous governors of Egypt who would typically have come from within the establishment in Istanbul, who would have been known there within the leading households, and for whom the governorship of Egypt would have been but a step in their advancement within the empire's bureaucracy, Mehmed Ali was a complete unknown quantity to the ruling factions of the capital. Besides all this, Egypt was too important a province to be entrusted to an outsider, and it was only a matter of time before Istanbul would have tried to remove him from this coveted position. These questions about how he was regarded in Istanbul must have caused deep anxiety for Mehmed Ali – an anxiety that was heightened by the fact that the investiture *firmans* were valid only for one year, and had to be renewed from year to year – making him wonder how long his tenure as governor of Egypt might last.

There were also important questions surrounding the three factions within Egypt that had brought him to Istanbul's attention, and which forced the sultan's hand into appointing him governor of Egypt. Each one of these three factions – namely the Albanians, the coalition of *ulama*/merchants, and the populace of Cairo – had its own problems and could very well turn against him at any moment. To start with, the Albanians were still loyal to him and saw their own rise within Egypt linked to *his* survival; however, experience had shown that they could be over-rebellious and capable of breaking into an open mutiny if they did not receive their regular pay, just as they had done under previous governors. Secondly, the *ulama*/ merchant coalition had been instrumental in pushing Istanbul to install him in Egypt, but these men had acted too independently and had in fact imposed on him serious conditions that curtailed his ability to raise taxes. Thirdly, the people of Cairo, by taking to the streets and tipping the balance of power in his favor against Hurşid during the crucial weeks of the summer of 1805, needed to be checked if their independent action was not to lead to complete anarchy.

THE ELIMINATION OF LOCAL RIVALS

With the *firman* of investiture in hand, Mehmed Ali set out systematically to get rid of his local rivals. His natural shrewdness allowed him to frustrate all attempts at forging a coalition among his rivals and always succeeded in driving a wedge between the different factions. Thus, the *ulama* never managed to agree with the Mamluks; the leading merchants were incapable of rallying the population of Cairo against the new pasha's policies; and the Albanians were always derided and hated by everyone. But this policy of *divide et impera* was not enough to establish his sole hegemony: Mehmed Ali would actively have to seek to weaken each one of these factions individually. As the backbone of his powerbase since he had arrived in Egypt, he assembled his fierce Albanian troops and dispatched them to fight the Mamluks in Upper Egypt. This weakened the Mamluks considerably, and it also depleted the energy of the Albanian troops, prompting many of them to contemplate returning home in order to bring an end to this fighting that never seemed to reach a conclusion. He also seized the opportunity of the ongoing war against the Wahhabis and sent many of these Albanians to meet their deaths in Arabia (which we shall return to later).

In 1806 Mehmed Ali launched his efforts to curtail the power of the *ulama* by placing one of their leading men, Shaykh Sharqawi, under house arrest. Given the social standing of the *ulama* and the important role they traditionally played in championing people's rights and acting as mediators between rulers and ruled, he could not afford a head-on confrontation with them. He therefore moved cautiously and curtailed their economic strength. In successive measures, he cancelled the tax exemptions that many of the shaykhs had enjoyed (in their capacity as *multazims*, or tax-farmers); he snatched villages from those whose taxes were not paid; and finally he targeted *rizqa*, or tax-free, lands that had been endowed for religious purposes mostly for the upkeep of mosques and *madrassas*. These repeated attacks on the privileges of religious men over a two-year period triggered their revolt in July 1809 which was led by none other than 'Umar Makram, who had played a key role in the uprising that had brought Mehmed Ali to power four years earlier. After repeated gatherings, petitions and remonstrations, the revolt failed and the popular shaykh was exiled to Damietta, only being allowed to return to Cairo years later once his popularity had been all but forgotten. With the loss of their leader and hopelessly divided in their stance against the Pasha, the *ulama* were effectively wiped out as serious opposition.

Mehmed Ali's efforts in consolidating his power against domestic rivals were briefly disrupted by two "outside" challenges that threatened to oust him from Egypt altogether. The first had occurred in June 1806, barely a year into his tenure as governor of Egypt, when news came through that the grand admiral had arrived in Alexandria accompanied by Musa Pasha, the ex-governor of Thessaloniki, who – as was typical of Istanbul's policy – was under instructions to switch posts with Mehmed Ali. When Mehmed Ali heard this news, he summoned his senior Albanian officers and informed them of the new *firman* and managed to convince them that his departure from Egypt meant their departure as well. It did not take much effort to persuade them to back his decision to defy the new orders from Istanbul, for, as aptly put by Jabarti,

> … there was not a man among them who had not acquired [in Egypt] a number of houses, wives, estates for tax-farming, and unbelievable power. It would never occur to such a man to allow himself to be stripped of such things, even if he had to risk death (Jabarti, 1994, IV, 14–15).

Mehmed Ali then went to the *ulama* and laid out in front of them their choices: either give their support to him, or back up Istanbul's new decree. If they went for the second option, he reminded them, they would effectively be returning to Mamluk rule. After mulling it over the *ulama* cast their lot in with him, and they wrote a detailed letter to the grand admiral informing him of why they could not agree with Istanbul's wish. When he realized that the force he had brought with him was insufficient to dislodge Mehmed Ali from Egypt and that the religious and popular leaders were throwing their lot in with him, the grand admiral had no choice but to leave, taking with him Musa Pasha to escort him back to his former position in Thessaloniki.

In the following year a more serious "outside" challenge confronted Mehmed Ali. While he was busy fighting the Mamluks in the south, news reached him that on 27 March 1807 some 5000 British troops had landed in Alexandria, captured the city and headed east to Rosetta. For a long time Mehmed Ali had been aware of secret negotiations between the British and the Mamluks and he feared that

landing with such a significant force could only mean that the British
wanted to hand the country over to their Mamluk allies. This was
devastating news coming as it did just when he thought he had managed to frustrate Istanbul's attempt to dislodge him from Egypt. He
soon lost heart and contemplated fleeing to Syria, formulating possible excuses he could make if Istanbul asked him why he had failed to
prevent the invasion. In a last desperate move, however, he changed
course and sent some shaykhs to the Mamluks suing for peace in the
hope that they would march with him against "the enemies of the
faith". After hours of negotiations the Mamluk leaders overcame
their inherent suspicions of the Pasha and started marching north
with him.

Before reaching Cairo, however, Mehmed Ali heard that the
British advance had been halted in Rosetta. It turned out that the governor of the town, Ali Bey al-Silanikli (i.e. the Thessalonikian), who
was a friend of Mehmed Ali's, had prepared a trap for the British in
town: seeing the gates of the town flung open, the British thought the
town had surrendered. They thus marched confidently through the
gates only to find themselves coming under fire from the residents
who aimed at them from the rooftops. Scores were killed, their heads
chopped off and sent to Cairo to be paraded on spikes. Others
were wounded or captured and were offered up for sale in the slave
market.

Irrespective of having contemplated fleeing to Syria when he
first heard of the British landing, or having taken part in any military
confrontations against them, Mehmed Ali still managed to claim
victory himself. This caused Jabarti to comment, with some irony, "If
only the people had been thanked for [putting up a fierce fight against
the British] or their actions acknowledged, but all the credit went to
the pasha and his soldiers" (Jabarti, 1994, IV, 79). With a large number of British prisoners of war under his control in the Citadel,
Mehmed Ali then opened negotiations with the British for their evacuation and oversaw their final departure from Alexandria in
September 1807.

Significantly, on finding the severed heads of the British displayed on spikes in Cairo, he ordered them to be buried after cutting off their ears and salting them. Then he ensured that these severed ears were sent to Istanbul both as a sign of his own triumph over his adversaries and to reiterate that he was always the obedient servant of the sultan and that whatever victories he accomplished they were all done in the name of his sovereign. In response the sultan sent him a personal *firman* in November 1807 and thanked him for his efforts in protecting Alexandria and for preventing the fall of Egypt into the hands of the "heathen English".

Mehmed Ali seized the opportunity to appoint his own man, Boghos Yousufian, to be governor of Alexandria and in so doing he reversed the Ottoman precedent of appointing the port's governor from Istanbul. Thus his control was now extended beyond the confines of Cairo to include this important city. An Armenian who would later become the Pasha's advisor for foreign affairs, Boghos counseled him to capitalize on the commercial opportunity which arose from the havoc caused by the Napoleonic wars in Europe, and the fact that British forces in Malta and Spain were in need of grain. The Pasha accepted his new governor's recommendation to supply the British swiftly with provisions that had been collected from the Delta. Growing in confidence with his newly extended reach of control, Mehmed Ali then went on to impose an export monopoly in grain and managed to reap considerable profits as a result. This was the beginning of what would later become a characteristic feature of his economic policy: establishing his control over the production of agricultural commodities and monopolizing both their internal and external trade.

In addition to strengthening the Pasha's hand vis-à-vis the *ulama*, these significant commercial profits also helped him in his confrontation with the leading merchants; those of them who were quick to realize which way the winds were blowing soon joined the Pasha's camp and effectively became employees in his service. Chief among them was Muhammad al-Mahruqi who had inherited a large fortune from his father and who ended up working for the Pasha requisitioning his troops.

THE MAMLUK MASSACRE

With these successive measures Mehmed Ali managed not only to augment his economic power significantly but also consolidated his political position by getting rid of his rivals. However, the Pasha still had to confront the single most important challenge to his hegemonic control, that of the Mamluks. In January 1807 the Pasha decided to confront these formidable enemies who had rallied behind one of their most senior grandees, al-Alfi Bey. On 27 January Mehmed Ali ordered all his troops to muster without delay and to cross the Nile near Cairo and to prepare for engagement to the north of Giza. However, when the two armies confronted each other and when the Mamluks saw Mehmed Ali riding among his soldiers they were so intimidated by this sight that they refused to fight! Al-Alfi tried to entice his men to attack but they would not budge. At a distance al-Alfi observed his adversary and exclaimed, "This is the *tahmaz* [or, the wise man] of the age! What else could it be?" (Jabarti, 1994, IV, 55). Admitting defeat without even a single musket being fired, he dismounted from his steed and walked aimlessly up a hill overlooking Cairo across the Nile. He then broke out in an emotional soliloquy that was to be his swan song:

> O Cairo, look at your children scattered about you, far from each
> other, dispersed, while there settle in you boorish Turks and Jews,
> and vile Albanians. They collect your revenues, wage war on your
> children, fight with your brave men, and contend with your horsemen.
> They tear down your houses, live in your palaces, ravish your sons and
> daughters, and blot out your beauty and light. (ibid.)

He was then seized by a fit and, with the realization that death was close, he gathered his retainers and told them, "It is all over. Cairo belongs to Mehmed Ali. There is no one who can challenge him. He has the Mamluks of Egypt in his power, and after today they will never again raise their standard." That night he died.

When the news came to Mehmed Ali of his rival's death he could not believe his ears, and with its confirmation he sighed and said,

"Now Egypt has become pleasant to me. I no longer have to worry about anyone else" (Jabarti, 1994, IV, 55–56).

However, the Mamluks, in spite of losing one of their most capable leaders, were not yet a spent force: they continued to ravage the countryside and divert a large portion of the country's revenue away from the Pasha. Again Mehmed Ali was anxious to end their nuisance once and for all, especially since he was receiving constant orders from Istanbul to prepare a military expedition against the Wahhabis in Arabia.

From as early as 1802 news had arrived from Najd in eastern Arabia that a tribal shaykh, Ibn Saʿud, had been defying Ottoman authority in the region, and that he had rapidly spread his control over all of the Hijaz; he had allied himself with a puritanical sect, the Wahhabis, that had been founded by Muhammad ibn ʿAbd al-Wahhab. When the Saʿudis and Wahhabis captured Mecca in 1803 and took control of Medina the following year – acts which caused obstruction to the annual pilgrimage – Istanbul considered this as a serious attack on Ottoman sovereignty, as well as a grave challenge to the prestige of the Ottoman sultan who had prided himself on being "The Protector of the two Holy Shrines". Orders were then dispatched to various provincial governors, including Mehmed Ali in Egypt, to send troops to fight the Wahhabis in Arabia and to return the Holy Cities to the Ottoman fold.

Responding to these orders entailed many risks. In addition to the obvious dangers of leading a military campaign on hostile enemy territory, the likelihood was that Mehmed Ali would also incur considerable expenses in raising and fitting out such a campaign. Furthermore, his departure from Egypt would provide a golden opportunity for Istanbul to replace him with a more trusted man to govern this important province. The Mamluks could also seize the same opportunity to regain some of the ground they had lost in their military confrontations with him. On the other hand, not obeying Istanbul's orders in this crucial mission would carry with it the dangers of being considered unreliable and untrustworthy, especially since he was still an unknown quantity in the Ottoman capital.

In other words, Istanbul's orders to fight the Wahhabis in Arabia presented Mehmed Ali with very bleak options – and the manner in which he dealt with these orders is testimony to his shrewd political mind. He procrastinated for a while and whenever he received fresh orders he would write back giving one justification or excuse after another. On one occasion it was the situation of the low Nile and the inability to incur any expenses necessary to prepare for the campaign; another time it was the Russo–Ottoman war and his fears that his departure from Egypt might provide the opportunity for one of the European powers to occupy Egypt and therefore disrupt the fragile balance of power in Europe. When he finally decided, after a lapse of several years, to obey Istanbul's orders he did so in a very artful manner. First of all, he informed Istanbul that he would not lead the campaign himself and requested that an official *firman* be sent appointing his second son, Tousson, by then a lad of only seventeen years old, to lead the campaign. When the *firman* arrived from Istanbul as requested, Mehmed Ali was determined to make use of the opportunity of the official ceremony in which it would be publicly announced to get rid of the Mamluks in one clean, decisive strike.

The Pasha then consulted his astrologers as to the most auspicious date on which to announce this *firman* and to proclaim it publicly. They told him that the fourth hour of Friday, 6 Safar 1226 (2 March 1811), would be the best time. Heralds were sent to the markets announcing, "*Yarin alay*", or "Tomorrow there will be a procession". On the eve of the procession Mehmed Ali sent notification to all Mamluk leaders – with whom he had reached a temporary truce allowing them to stay in Cairo – inviting them to the Citadel with their retainers to witness the official bestowal of the command of the Hijaz campaign on his son Tousson and cloaking him with the ceremonial robe. He pleaded that his son would be honored to have the Mamluk leaders march with him through the streets of Cairo after receiving the full regalia from his father; the Mamluks were therefore told to arrive attired in their ceremonial robes in the Citadel at the auspicious hour set by the astrologers.

Not realizing that this "auspicious hour" would be the hour of their death, the Mamluks ascended in great pomp and ceremony to the Pasha in his *divan*, or council chamber, in the Citadel. After spending an hour drinking coffee with him, the leaders left in a procession that descended again in the prescribed manner and passed through a narrow path that led down to the city. After all the troops had passed through a certain gate, an order was given to close that gate, trapping the Mamluk beys with all their retainers in the narrow pathway. The Pasha's soldiers were then ordered to open fire and to spare no one. The shooting went on for an hour, killing over four hundred and fifty Mamluk beys; the heads were severed from the corpses and displayed to Mehmed Ali who by then had retired to his harem. The bloodbath continued in the city below as the Pasha's soldiers were unleashed into the Mamluks' households where they pillaged their property, raped their women and killed any remaining Mamluk who dared to hide.

The sinister scheme was executed flawlessly and one can see the hand of Mehmed Lazoğlu, Mehmed Ali's trusted and loyal deputy, behind it. Key to its success was the utmost secrecy in which it was shrouded; so secretive was it that it was rumored that besides the Pasha, only three people had been informed of it. Not even the Pasha's sons, Tousson and Ibrahim, got wind of it. And, unlike the earlier, much clumsier attempt in October 1801 by the Ottoman grand vizier and the grand admiral to execute a similar massacre, this time there was no British navy to come to the rescue of what Jabarti called the "Egyptian princes". What helped make this massacre the decisive end to the Mamluk presence in Egypt, was that those Mamluks who had escaped it by being fortunate enough not to be in Cairo on that "auspicious" day, were mercilessly hunted down by Mehmed Ali's eldest son, Ibrahim Bey. In the months that followed the Citadel massacre he chased them from village to village in Upper Egypt killing no less than a thousand Mamluks in the process.

By instigating the Mamluk massacre Mehmed Ali was now the uncontested ruler of his adopted homeland. Ten years after landing in Egypt and six years after being appointed as its governor he was now sole hegemon in what he considered his new country. During these ten years he had managed to get rid of the irksome popular leadership that had been instrumental in bringing him to power; he had curtailed the strength of the religious leaders through taxing their lands and cutting down their financial privileges; and above all he had managed through one clean and decisive strike to eliminate all competing rivals in Egypt. Finally, through his greater control over agricultural development and lucrative trade opportunities with Europe, he had gradually succeeded in augmenting his own personal wealth.

Mehmed Ali, in spite of these significant achievements, still had deep anxieties about the security of his position. As we shall see, the manner in which he successfully dealt with these anxieties further consolidated his role in Egypt and dictated his policies, both within Egypt and abroad, and in the process transformed the very character of Egyptian society.

ENTRENCHMENT

Immediately after eliminating the Mamluks, Mehmed Ali sent a long letter to Istanbul in which he characterized his act as an implementation of the Sultan's old desire to strengthen his control over Egypt. He was obviously aware that people in the capital were questioning his loyalty and speculating as to the increasingly independent posture he was assuming. Until now he had managed to walk the tightrope between acknowledging the sultan's overall suzerainty while practically pursuing his own independent policies. But for how long could he maintain this delicate balancing act? And for how long would Istanbul allow him to have this room for maneuver before deciding to seize the initiative from him? The news of the mutiny that occurred in 1807 in the Ottoman capital that cost Sultan Selim III his throne and then his life might have provided Mehmed Ali with some respite, for it kept Istanbul off his back for a while. However, this proved to be a blessing in disguise – for the new sultan, Mahmud II, showed a clear determination to establish Istanbul's firm control over distant and recalcitrant provinces. Mehmed Ali's decision to dispatch the Hijaz campaign, led by his own son, was an attempt to placate Istanbul and allay its suspicions of him and to prove that he was, indeed, the loyal, subservient servant that was expected of a provincial governor.

BUILDING AN ALTERNATIVE POWERBASE

Irrespective of the importance of placating Istanbul by launching campaigns in its name, Mehmed Ali's chances of survival in Egypt depended on founding a loyal elite to replace the old aristocracy that he had decimated. Traditionally, Mamluk warlords had perpetuated their presence in Egypt by replenishing their numbers through fresh imports of slaves from Georgia. Unlike the Mamluk beys, Mehmed Ali was a freeborn Muslim and he could draw upon members of his immediate and extended family to assist him in running Egypt as his large, personal fief. And it was this expertise in building a household centered around members of his family and around friends and acquaintances from his hometown, Kavala, and its environs, that was another of the many signs of his wide-ranging talents. This chapter follows the Pasha in his attempts to construct such a household, identifies key members of the household, and traces the Pasha's efforts in using this new elite to further his policies during the second decade of his life in Egypt from 1811 to 1821.

A mere month after being officially instated by the sultan as governor of Egypt in 1805, Mehmed Ali summoned his two eldest sons, Ibrahim and Tousson, to Egypt and immediately appointed them in senior posts in spite of their young age. Ibrahim was first appointed as governor of the Citadel when he was only sixteen years old. Four years later his younger brother, Tousson, by then seventeen years old, was appointed head of the military campaign against the Wahhabis in Arabia.

In 1809, furthermore, Mehmed Ali thought it was time to summon his wife, Emine, and his other children, Ismail, Tevhide and Nazlı, to Egypt. This in itself was not a novel move as previous Ottoman governors had been in the habit of bringing their harem with them. What was unusual with Mehmed Ali however was that by summoning his family to Egypt it became apparent that he intended to stay there for good, for there is evidence that he started to build a family mausoleum in south-eastern Cairo as early as 1808. This was a striking decision for by that time he had not yet got rid of the

Mamluks nor had he accomplished any of the great achievements for which his reign became renowned. So this early decision to construct a mausoleum in Egypt clearly demonstrates that Mehmed Ali had every confidence that he and his family would remain there until their deaths.

After settling his immediate family in Egypt, Mehmed Ali invited other distant relatives to come and live in his new country, and eventually uncles and aunts, nephews and nieces, cousins and friends flocked to Egypt in droves and were given important positions, lucrative stipends and fancy mansions. Examples of these relatives included the Yeğen siblings (four brothers and two sisters) who, as their name indicates – *Yeğen* in Turkish means nephew / niece – were the Pasha's nephews and nieces. Two of them, Ibrahim and Ahmed, would later occupy senior military posts and would be appointed as governors of dominions brought under the Pasha's control (Yemen and Arabia, respectively). Yet another nephew, Mehmed Şerif, arrived from Kavala to be given one important post after another. He was first appointed as the Pasha's deputy, then as governor of lower Egypt, then as governor general of Syria after it had been incorporated into his uncle's dominions, then as director of the Pasha's cabinet, and finally as director of finances. To further consolidate his household and to reinforce the connection it had with Kavala, Mehmed Ali ensured that his sisters and daughters would marry men from his hometown, and then invited these new members of his wider family to Egypt. Foremost among these in-laws was Müharrem Bey who was originally from Kavala and was married to Mehmed Ali's eldest daughter, Tevhide. Müharrem Bey eventually became governor of Alexandria and then commander-in-chief of his father-in-law's navy. The Pasha's second daughter, Nazlı, was married to Mehmed Hüsrev Dramallı who, as his name indicates, was from the town of Drama to the north of Kavala. He would eventually be appointed as treasurer and hence be known in this capacity as Mehmed Bey Defterdar (*defterdar* meaning treasurer). A third daughter, Zeyneb, was married to Ahmed Abu Widan, a former Circassian slave of Mehmed Ali who would later be appointed as director of war and then governor general of the Sudan. Mehmed Ali's uncle, Ishaq, was also invited to Egypt. His daughter, Nebihe, was married to Osman Nureddin who would later be appointed in charge of the navy.

AN ECONOMIC POLICY TAKES SHAPE

There were droves of other men who flocked to the Pasha's service after hearing of the lucrative stipends they could receive in Egypt. As we have seen, the Pasha's increased wealth was partly due to the tight trade monopoly policy he instituted during his early years as governor. In 1811 the sale of the entire cereal production of Upper Egypt was monopolized. In the following year he extended this to the rice production of the Delta, and in 1815 it was the turn of sugar from Upper Egypt. By 1816 Mehmed Ali had extended this policy to most of the country's cash crops. This allowed him to buy these crops from the peasants at prices below their market level and reap significant profits after selling them domestically or on the international market.

In addition, and soon after getting rid of the Mamluks, Mehmed Ali was able to confiscate the *iltizam*s (tax-farms) whereby the right to collect the land tax had been sold to those who could pay the tax amount in advance: *iltizam*s of Upper Egypt were abolished in 1812 and those of Lower Egypt in 1814. Soon thereafter agricultural *waqf*s (land whose revenue was allocated for religious purposes, such as the maintenance of mosques, schools, etc.) were also confiscated. Having thus extended his control over the proprietorship of land, the process of tax collection, and the sale of agricultural produce, Mehmed Ali then moved one step further in controlling the agricultural sector by interfering in the actual production process. He introduced new crops and new techniques and established a system of crop rotation with which the peasants were forced to comply.

These successive measures, while allowing Mehmed Ali to control the agricultural surplus in a way that no previous Ottoman governor had ever managed to do, had a heavy impact on the poor, both in the cities and in the countryside. Realizing that their own livelihoods were being controlled and manipulated by the Pasha's increasingly sophisticated and tight administrative machinery, they started thinking of themselves as working directly for the Pasha. When a local tax farmer, for example, attempted to collect taxes from some peasants, they responded by saying "Your days are over, and we have become the Pasha's peasants!" (Jabarti, 1994, IV, 289). Their occasional attempts to do business the old way were met with brutality by the Pasha's agents. Ali Silanikli, for example, whom we saw earlier repulsing the British attack on Rosetta, was rumored to arrest peasants who were caught selling cloth on the open market instead of forwarding it, as per orders, to the Pasha's warehouses, and to wrap them in the same cloth after soaking it in tar and setting fire to them ('Arif, n.d., II, fols. 72–73). (As a sign of his closeness to Mehmed Ali and how much the Pasha thought of him as a member of his household, Ali Silanikli was buried in the Pasha's own mausoleum after he died in 1824.)

In Cairo, the Pasha's market inspector was legendarily harsh in meeting any deviations from the Pasha's regulations: currency counterfeiters were hanged from one of the old gates of medieval Cairo with coins clipped to their noses; butchers caught cheating in the weight of meat had their noses slit with pieces of meat hanging from them; and pastry merchants caught for a similar crime were forced to sit on their hot pans while still on the fire (Jabarti, 1994, IV, 391–393).

At the same time, the Pasha's coffers were being regularly replenished and it did not take much time for the rumor to spread throughout the four corners of the Ottoman Empire that Mehmed Ali's treasury was brimming over with money ('Arif, n.d., II, fol. 42). With his fast increasing wealth Mehmed Ali was able to cement the elite he was gradually building in Egypt, and by extending generous offers to men who flocked to work for him from throughout the Empire he was in a position to compete with the sultan. He once told a French advisor, "Fortunately, he [the sultan] pays small salaries. I have paid far more ..." However, if the sultan could count on the weight of his title and his royal pedigree, Mehmed Ali had to take extreme measures to make sure that those whom he attracted remained loyal to him, and what better way to secure their loyalty than to make them wholly dependent on him? "It has been necessary to keep them faithful to me," he told the same French advisor. "I have found the way to do so by lavishing upon them money and presents but preventing them becoming proprietors [of agricultural land] and creating for themselves a personal influence over the population" (Douin, 1927, 111). As a result, Mehmed Ali came to be known among members of this privileged elite as *veli nimet* (Ar. *waliyy al-ni'am*), a title which had traditionally been used by the Ottoman sultans and one which literally means "source of benefaction" or simply, "benefactor". It soon became one of the most common titles by which Mehmed Ali was known, one that was dearest to his heart.

THE HIJAZ CAMPAIGN

Feeling more and more secure in his new home as a result of this close-knit elite he had woven around himself, Mehmed Ali started to pursue policies that no previous Ottoman governor could even have contemplated. His policy of summoning friends and relatives and appointing them in key positions domestically raised eyebrows in the Ottoman capital with more and more viziers whispering about what his secret goals might be. Yet, lacking an effective fighting force and seeing that this controversial governor showed no signs of outright rebellion, Istanbul was content to give this mysterious pasha the benefit of the doubt.

When he received his orders to launch the campaign against the Wahhabis in 1811 Mehmed Ali could not afford to lose this first test of loyalty. He therefore did his best to supply his son Tousson who was leading the campaign with as many men and as much supplies and ammunition as he could muster. He also appointed Sayyid Muhammad al-Mahruqi as quartermaster of the campaign and urged his son to consult with him regularly. Mehmed Ali hoped that his son's youth and inexperience could be offset by having Mahruqi next to him and by he himself supervising the complex process of supplying and paying the 15,000-strong army.

At the same time he stayed in touch with his son with letters of encouragement to boost his morale and give him sound advice. The relationship between father and son comes across from these letters as an intimate and affectionate one, and in spite of the increasingly formalistic forms of address that each used, one can feel the close bond between both men. When for example, he heard that the army had suffered a minor defeat, Mehmed Ali wrote to his son saying,

> His Excellency, my most beloved and honored son, Tousson Pasha ... Victory and defeat come from God and are in His hands. So ... [my son] the pupil of my eye, don't give up and don't despair, for despair is a disgrace not befitting you, and it is wrong for despondency to creep into your heart. Know that courage and bravery entail attacking the enemy again, and again taking revenge on him. I have a lot of equipment and money, thanks to the Sultan, which I will send to you promptly. So don't be sad and always be on your guard ... And don't forget that I, myself, have sometimes been victorious and at other times the enemy has inflicted me with setbacks, and that I have been disturbed by this, but that I have always fought back and destroyed the enemy. (Egyptian National Archives, 1812)

After eighteen months of fighting, Tousson managed to expel the Wahhabis from Medina in December 1812. Mehmed Ali immediately sent Latif Ağa, his key-bearer, to Istanbul with the keys of the city and 300 pairs of ears that had been torn from the bodies of the dead Wahhabi chieftains. The news was received with extreme jubilation in Istanbul and even Hüsrev Pasha, now back in the Ottoman capital, had to swallow his pride and write to his old rival congratulating him on this significant victory.

The following month (January 1813) Tousson captured Mecca and he wrote to his father saying that he had managed to visit the Grand Mosque and Ibrahim's tomb in Mecca. Some thirty-one Meccan *ulama* wrote to Mehmed Ali thanking him for cleansing the Holy City of the "heretic, violent, belligerent ... atheist" Wahhabis (Egyptian National Archives, 1813). Mehmed Ali, keen to show his loyalty to the sultan, spared no time in sending his third son, Ismail, then seventeen years old, to Istanbul with the key of the Holy City. This was no small achievement and the sultan, to show his personal appreciation of his vassal, honored Ismail with a grand reception to which all the viziers were summoned. In a very rare gesture the sultan even appeared in person and received the key of the city with his own hands. To reward Tousson for returning the Holy Cities to the Ottoman fold and for thus restoring the prestige of the sultan, Sultan Mahmud bestowed the governorship of Jeddah on him. He also appointed him as Shaykh of Mecca. Of equal significance for Mehmed Ali was a *firman* he received informing him that a *fetva* (a religious ruling in Islamic law) had been issued allowing Sultan Mahmud to add the title "*Ghazi*", or Warrior/Conqueror, to his many titles in recognition of his victory over the Wahhabis.

This was a great honor and Mehmed Ali must have felt enormous pride that it was thanks to him that the sultan could add such a coveted title to his name. He had now become one of the most powerful governors within the empire and it might have been construed that the sultan owed him a personal favor. Emboldened by this recognition, he wrote to his agent in Istanbul, Necib Efendi (Ar. Najib Afandi), asking him to intercede on his behalf and to request to be granted the right to collect the taxes of the entire island of Thasos off the shore of his native town of Kavala. Considering himself to be on a par with the grandest Ottoman grandees, he promised to use the proceeds of the island's taxes to build a huge educational establishment for the poor of Kavala and its environs. In response, the sultan allowed him to establish an endowment (*waqf*) from the revenue of Thasos. This *waqf* was to be used to build a vast educational complex that included a primary and a secondary school, an *imaret*, or soup kitchen, for feeding the poor and needy, a mosque and a *hammam*. The *imaret* of Mehmed Ali, as it came to be known, had the capacity to lodge over 100 students and to provide them with free education and food for the duration of their stay. This was the earliest and, by all accounts, the largest educational establishment that Mehmed Ali was to build.

Back in Arabia, it was not long before Tousson's troops suffered serious setbacks and it was clear to Mehmed Ali that his son could not handle all the logistical, financial and military affairs of the campaign, let alone master the complex issues of Arabian tribal politics that were necessary if he were to have an edge over the Wahhabis on their own territory. After some deliberation Mehmed Ali took the bold decision to go to Arabia in person. He must have weighed the risks involved in leaving Egypt against the benefits of his personal presence in Arabia, and the need to ensure that all his efforts that had been incurred in the Hijaz campaign were not in vain. During the nearly two years he spent in Arabia from August 1813 to June 1815 he managed to reshuffle various administrative positions by dismissing some governors whose loyalty to his household was suspect. He also negotiated with tribal chieftains to cast their lot in with him and to turn against the Sa'udis. While in Arabia he performed the pilgrimage and from henceforth acquired the title "*Hajji*".

Although he could not defeat the Wahhabis decisively, Tousson finally wrote and asked his father if he could return to Egypt. He had gained the reputation of being generous and courageous and was genuinely fond of the Egyptians, and he in turn was loved and respected by his men, so it was to a hero's welcome that he came back on his return to Egypt. On 29 September 1816, he retired to his palace and prepared for a joyful celebration. No sooner had the festivities begun however than he fell ill with bubonic plague and within twenty-four hours he was dead. When his father heard the devastating news he was completely overcome. By this time Tousson's funeral cortège was already on its way to the mausoleum in Cairo which the Pasha had had constructed for himself and his family. The Pasha joined it, distraught and confused, and unable to take in what had happened.

After recovering from this personal tragedy, Mehmed Ali was determined to finish off what Tousson had left behind in Arabia. He sent his eldest son, Ibrahim, to resume the fight against the Wahhabis and their Sa'udi allies. This gave Ibrahim the opportunity to prove his military acumen with a proficiency that was due as much to his bold tactical moves and his ability to seize the initiative as to his mastery of the crucial questions of morale, logistics and supply. His master-stroke on the Arabian battlefield was his successful siege of Dar'iyya, the Sa'udi capital. On 16 September 1818 and with orders from his father he allowed his soldiers to sack the city and raze it to the ground. He then arrested the Sa'udi leader, 'Abdallah ibn Sa'ud, and sent him bound in chains to his father in Egypt; from there Mehmed Ali sent him on to Istanbul where he was beheaded on 17 December 1818. Once again Sultan Mahmud acknowledged his indebtedness to Mehmed Ali by issuing a *firman* which appointed his son Ibrahim to the governorship of Jeddah and officially bestowed on him the title of Pasha.

As well as being a testimony to his military skills Ibrahim's un-ambiguous victory in Arabia and his destruction of the first Sa'udi state also owes something to Mehmed Ali's ability to requisition the troops with their pay and salaries (even though not always on time). This was to become a regular feature of Mehmed Ali's long reign whereby a "division of labor" was devised between father and son which allowed Ibrahim to concentrate on military aspects, while Mehmed Ali took care of the financial, logistical and diplomatic aspects of these military confrontations.

It is interesting to note with respect to the Arabian campaign that in addition to the logistical and financial support that Mehmed Ali provided, Ibrahim's military success was dependent on the earlier administrative experience he had gained in Egypt when he helped his father perform a complete overhaul of the Egyptian countryside. In the wake of the Mamluk massacre Mehmed Ali appointed Ibrahim, who had been acting as his chief accountant since 1807, as governor of Upper Egypt and succeeded in securing a *firman* from the sultan confirming this appointment. In his new capacity Ibrahim managed to extend his father's control over all the territory in the south, conduct a survey of these lands, and subject the surveyed land to a higher tax rate. The following year, 1814, territory in the Delta was similarly surveyed, and the extremely detailed and meticulous manner in which the survey was conducted allowed the Pasha to offset the losses he had incurred from his trade with Europe and also to defray the rising cost of the war in Arabia. Later, in 1821, Ibrahim helped to supervise yet another cadastre and when he became aware that two sets of land surveyors were producing different results, one slow and accurate, and the other faster but less accurate, he insisted on combining precision with speed.

ABSOLUTE POWER

Ibrahim displayed a brutality and ruthlessness to the peasants, *multazims* (tax-farmers), and village shaykhs that was not so very different from the manner in which he dealt with his enemies on the battlefield. Jabarti could not hide his indignation in describing the atrocities committed by Ibrahim in Upper Egypt that included roasting a peasant who could not pay his taxes like skewered meat over a pit. The perceptive chronicler even compared Ibrahim's ruthless tactics to the proverbial atrocities committed by the Tatars in the thirteenth and fourteenth centuries (Jabarti, 1994, IV, 256).

It was not only Ibrahim who overstepped limits through his reliance on his relationship to the Pasha: abuse of power was endemic and inherent in the very system the Pasha had established. A household government is, by necessity, a corrupt one, and there are many incidents that indicate that the members of the Pasha's immediate household often exceeded their limits only to be admonished by Mehmed Ali when he found out. There is the story, for example, of Hüseyin, one of Mehmed Ali's sons, who found the school he was sent to in Giza rather cold. He therefore asked for a heater to be brought to him. When his father heard about the incident, he reprimanded his key-bearer who had responded to the young man's request. The key-bearer replied saying, "What can I do? At a time when we answer similar requests by strangers, am I supposed to refuse the wishes of Mehmed Ali's son?" ('Arif, n.d., II, fol. 67). Then there is the story of the Pasha's daughter, Nazlı, who was married to the chief treasurer, Mehmed Bey Defterdar. She was said to have been deeply in love with her husband and also to be jealously possessive of him. One day when he happened to remark on the beauty of one of his female slaves, Nazlı listened quietly. Later at dinner she presented him with the head of the slave girl on a serving dish. He got up from the table and went out, never to return to her (Tugay, 1963, 117). When Mehmed Ali heard about the incident he was so enraged that he ordered his grandson, Abbas, to kill his aunt but after prolonged pleas from Abbas, Mehmed Ali agreed to spare his daughter's life.

TIGHTENING THE SCREW

Thus it was that Mehmed Ali demonstrated his dependence on his closest kin to push for his policies in Egypt and beyond. Gradually his family emerged as the epicenter of power in Egypt and the members of the new elite that was being forged around it came to measure their importance according to their distance from this family. To strengthen his position further Mehmed Ali had to keep a close eye on how his chosen circle behaved and, more importantly, to catch any murmur of conspiracy that Istanbul might have been hatching against him domestically. His chief agent in this respect was Mehmed Lazoğlu who entered his service in 1810 and subsequently became his deputy two years later. He was known to possess a ruthless character and to have his fingers in many pies throughout Egypt. His power derived from Mehmed Ali's unbounded trust in him and, in turn, he did a lot of the Pasha's dirty work. Chief among his accomplishments was putting in place a complex spy network that allowed him to foil many a plot against his patron. The network involved countless agents who disguised themselves as street vendors and roamed the various districts of Cairo at night hoping to be invited into the houses of the rich and powerful. Once inside they would feign ignorance of Turkish and snoop on the conversations taking place therein. They would then transcribe what they had overheard and deposit a nightly report at a certain secret address, all this without ever being aware of their fellow conspirators or meeting up with their chiefs. Their immediate superior, it turned out, was an old woman who was bilingual in Arabic and Turkish and who used to give Arabic lessons to Mehmed Ali. This woman would then gather these reports and after summarizing and distilling them, would forward a synopsis to Lazoğlu the following morning.

In 1815 Lazoğlu's system of information gathering proved crucially successful in uncovering a serious plot against Mehmed Ali. While the Pasha was in Arabia assisting Tousson in the fight against the Wahhabis he had sent his key-bearer, Latif Ağa, to present the key of Medina to the sultan in Istanbul. This same Latif Ağa was encouraged – probably by Mehmed Ali's old enemy Hüsrev – to turn against his master in Cairo. The title of Pasha was given to Latif Ağa and it was promised that if he managed to stage a palace coup, he would be given the governorship of Egypt instead of Mehmed Ali. On arrival in Egypt Latif seized the opportunity of Mehmed Ali's absence and started planning to depose the Pasha. Lazoğlu soon heard of the plot and immediately sent his men to arrest Latif Ağa and without even interrogating him, had him beheaded in the square at the foot of the Citadel. When Mehmed Ali returned from Arabia he approved of what Lazoğlu had done. He inquired, however, if Lazoğlu was certain of the accusations against Latif and asked him why he had not interrogated Latif before executing him. "If I had done so," Lazoğlu replied, "it would have been my head that would be chopped off instead" ('Arif, n.d., I, fol. 48; Jabarti, 1994, IV, 251–255).

INVESTING IN INFRASTRUCTURE

Even although Mehmed Ali was lacking the military might that could help to protect him from being ousted from his coveted province, he now had an ever growing sense of security in his position and a greater confidence that Istanbul had been placated by his victory in Arabia. Perhaps now was the time to contemplate undertaking huge changes to the country's infrastructure, which would also have the benefit of increasing revenue. Given their very nature, any improvements to the infrastructure would have been difficult for his predecessors to contemplate, let alone execute, as these governors were always aware that their tenure in Egypt would not last more than a few years.

We have already seen the collaboration on one such project between Mehmed Ali and his son Ibrahim, namely, the land survey that was conducted in 1813–1814. During his second decade in Egypt the Pasha ordered renewed excavation to deepen the canal that linked Alexandria to the Nile and was assisted in this huge project by Pascal Coste, a French architect from Marseille. Coste had come to Egypt in 1817 and was entrusted with many projects, among them the construction of several palaces for the Pasha in Cairo and Alexandria, a saltpeter factory in the Delta and a gunpowder store in Cairo; but it was the canal link between Alexandria and the Nile that was to be his chief accomplishment. Begun in 1817, the project took three years to be finished, and, when complete, the canal extended for some 72 kilometers, costing the Pasha some 35,000 purses (around 7.5 million francs). The whole undertaking was clear evidence of the extent to which he had managed to control the manpower resources of Egypt: reports estimate that around 300,000 workers were dragged in to work on the project. However, close to one-third of these workers perished in the process, due mainly to exhaustion, starvation and lack of medical services. To appease Istanbul, Mehmed Ali decided the new canal should carry the name "the Mahmudiyya", after the reigning Ottoman monarch, Sultan Mahmud II.

LINGERING ANXIETIES

In spite of his renewed sense of security in Egypt, Mehmed Ali still had to worry about his relationship with Istanbul as the possibility of confrontation with the sultan became ever more likely. News arriving from the capital indicated how keen Sultan Mahmud was to centralize Istanbul's rule and to tighten its grip over rebellious or recalcitrant provinces. Curiously, many of the sultan's policies were inspired by those of his ambitious governor in Egypt, and the decisive question became how Mehmed Ali could beat the sultan in this process of "reform".

Key to his success in this implicit struggle with Istanbul was his ability to create a fighting force that could frustrate any attempt to snatch Egypt away from him. Latif Aǧa's conspiracy made it clear that he had to be constantly on his guard. Moreover, the Arabian campaign highlighted to him that in spite of its successes on the battlefield, his army was unreliable, composed as it was of a mishmash of Albanian, Moroccan, Turkish and Bedouin elements. Immediately after his return from Arabia, therefore, he set about reorganizing his troops. Probably inspired by the example of the *nizam-i cedid* troops who had arrived in Egypt with the grand admiral Hüseyin Pasha in 1801, and perhaps with Hüsrev's earlier experiment also in mind when he attempted to implement these military reforms during his short tenure as governor of Egypt in 1802–1803, Mehmed Ali gathered his Albanian soldiers one hot day in August 1815 and ordered them to carry out target practice in the large square at the foot of the Citadel. The following day it was rumored that the Pasha wanted to conduct a headcount of the soldiers and to organize them along the lines of the *nizam-i cedid*.

The attempt failed miserably. The soldiers reluctantly complied with the Pasha's orders on the first day only to conspire to kill him the following night. Thanks to the efficiency of Lazoǧlu's spy network the Pasha was informed of the plot just in the nick of time and was speedily escorted to the Citadel. As soon as the conspirators realized their plan had been foiled, they went on the rampage in the streets of Cairo, looting and damaging a considerable amount of property. Mehmed Ali was only able to pacify the merchants and the populace by agreeing to return their stolen property or to compensate them for the damages they had suffered.

Mehmed Ali was deeply shaken by this serious incident which only served to emphasize the need for a reliable body of troops but, putting these thoughts aside for a while, he concentrated on matters closer to home. After five years, in 1820, he assembled and dispatched two expeditions to the Sudan, one under the command of his now twenty-five-year-old son, Ismail Pasha, and the other under the command of his son-in-law, Mehmed Bey Defterdar. The two expeditions numbered around 10,000 men and were composed of Moroccans, Bedouins, Albanian and Turks. Mehmed Ali's instructions to his son clearly stated that the main purpose of the campaign was to capture as many Sudanese as possible in order to conscript them into a new army he intended to create. "The value of slaves who prove to be suitable for our services is more precious than jewels ... Hence I am ordering you to collect 6000 of these slaves" (Egyptian National Archives, 1822).

The campaigns failed miserably in their prime objectives as the number of slaves captured was far less than the number hoped for. Furthermore, no serious thinking had gone into how to secure those who had been captured during their transportation to Egypt; in addition to which many perished on the long march north. And, to top it all, Ismail's command proved to be disastrous as many of his generals deserted him in his time of need and, in the end, Ismail was himself killed in a brutal incident. When news of this tragedy reached Mehmed Ali he decided to cut his losses and abandoned the whole idea of conscripting Sudanese for the disciplined army he had wanted to create.

COMMERCIAL SUCCESSES

The cost to Mehmed Ali of waging these repeated campaigns, plus the huge infrastructure projects, were not inconsiderable and necessitated a steady flow of income. His ability to pay for these expenses was due to the strict implementation of his monopolies policy which allowed him to divert the enormous proceeds of the country's agricultural and commercial sectors into his own coffers. Helping him in his commercial transactions with European merchants was Boghos Yousufiyan, the Armenian advisor we encountered earlier. Boghos was born in Izmir in 1768 and, apart from his mother tongue, he also spoke fluent Turkish, Greek, Italian and French. He arrived in Rosetta in 1790 and quickly became involved in commercial activities there. After a brief period of absence during the French occupation he returned to Egypt and entered Mehmed Ali's service. He was appointed to be in charge of the customs house in Alexandria and handled Mehmed Ali's expanding commercial interests in Europe.

A story illustrating the relationship between both men also gives an insight into how Mehmed Ali chose his close advisors. Sometime in 1813 an accountant whom Mehmed Ali had sent to Alexandria reported that Boghos had been embezzling the Pasha's treasury, whereupon Boghos was immediately summoned to meet the Pasha. After a brief interrogation he was found guilty and Mehmed Ali ordered him to be beheaded. It so happened, though, that the executioner had known Boghos previously and was indebted to him, given that Boghos had saved him from a life-threatening situation in the past. So, rather than kill him the executioner had him hidden in his own river-boat under the protection of his wife. A short while later when confronted with some tough financial quandary Mehmed Ali longed to be able to consult Boghos's expertise and wished that he had not ordered him to be put to death. On hearing this, the executioner told him that he had defied the original order and that Boghos was indeed alive and well and, so doing, he threw himself at the Pasha's feet begging for forgiveness. Magnanimously, Mehmed Ali gestured to him to fetch Boghos. As soon as he laid his eyes on Boghos, Mehmed Ali calmed down and entered into the financial deal at hand as if nothing had happened. And from then on Boghos became a pillar in Mehmed Ali's administration with overall responsibility for handling his commercial affairs and advising the Pasha on key matters of foreign policy. He is reported not to have changed his lifestyle or to have worn anything but a simple black robe throughout his life. In the thirty-four years he served Mehmed Ali, Boghos invited many of his relatives to settle in Egypt, assigning them important financial positions in the expanding bureaucracy and eventually becoming the doyen of a large and prosperous Armenian community.

After Boghos died in 1844 and they were going through his belongings, several *cartes blanches* with Mehmed Ali's seal, dating as far back as 1837 when the Pasha had undertaken a trip to the Sudan, were still found to be in his possession; it thus became clear to everyone just how trustworthy Boghos had been, given that he could have used these documents at any time to draw any sum of money for himself. When Mehmed Ali heard the news of his trusted friend's death and that his interment had already taken place in great haste, he wrote to the governor of Alexandria addressing him as "Donkey, brute", and ordered him to exhume the body so that Boghos could be dignified with an official funeral with full military honors.

Another man who was instrumental in reinforcing Mehmed Ali's control over the country during the early years of his reign was Mu'allim Ghali, a Copt who had been appointed as head of the corporation of accountants. Coptic scribes had been in charge of finances for centuries and they had assisted both the Mamluk beys and French administrators in assessing and collecting taxes. Soon after assuming power Mehmed Ali employed Ghali in this capacity and came to depend on him to inform him on all financial and landholding matters. Ever suspicious however, Mehmed Ali ordered Lazoğlu to arrest Ghali after he had heard rumors that Ghali had been embezzling money. Lazoğlu had Ghali brought in front of the Pasha and when Ghali could not produce the missing 6000 purses, Mehmed Ali had Ghali's brother, Fransis, and his accountant, Sim'an, fetched and they were lashed on the soles of their feet in front of him. He then ordered Ghali himself to be beaten. After receiving more than 1000 lashes Sim'an did not survive the beating; Fransis was told that he would be released to find a way to fetch the missing money and, if unsuccessful, his brother would remain in custody.

After his release, Ghali continued to assist Mehmed Ali in financial affairs but it seems his growing power and manner of conducting business clashed with Ibrahim Pasha, Mehmed Ali's son, who was building a powerbase of his own. In the end Ghali was assassinated and his body was dumped in the Nile. His son, Basilyus, inherited his post and continued to serve Mehmed Ali for years to come.

"THE OLD SPIDER IN HIS DEN"

During his years in office Mehmed Ali had contrived to form a loyal and trusted elite around him with these and many others of the men who served him. At the center of this elite was his own family household, and at the center of this intimate group was the Pasha himself: his actual physical presence, his words of command – whether issued verbally or transmitted in writing – and ultimately his every desire. At the beginning of his tenure Mehmed Ali could be seen wandering the streets of Cairo, visiting merchants and leading dignitaries and making himself visible for the commoners to gaze upon and to marvel at the pomp and ceremony with which he was surrounded – just as they had marveled at the elaborate parades of the Mamluks and the previous Ottoman governors. Gradually, however, Mehmed Ali had palaces constructed wherein he installed himself in ever more seclusion. Significantly, all his palaces were built in an Ottoman Rococo style and he ensured that they were designed and fitted out in a similar style to the palaces of Istanbul.

It was in these Cairene palaces that Mehmed Ali preferred to be seen. On reading the accounts of how he introduced himself to his European and Ottoman audiences, one can see the gradual progression of what was to become the most sophisticated of rituals; these were intended to instill a sense of the extraordinary in the minds of his visitors, and to show that the individual into whose presence they were about to enter was no ordinary man. It is related that his court, with its elaborate ceremonial practices, radiated fear and wonder in some mysterious and awe-inspiring fashion. Two themes, both related to light and visibility, could be discerned from these accounts of audiences with the Pasha – "the old spider in his den", in the words of one British traveler (Lindsay, 1838, I, 34).

The first one is a consistent reference to a dimly lit audience chamber, where thick brown candles cast long shadows, and where a sense of mystery was pervasive. After being escorted up the long incline to the Citadel and then through one crowded ante-chamber after another, the visitor would eventually find himself in the middle of a large hall devoid of all furniture except a broad divan extending the length of three of its four walls, in one corner of which emerging from the shadows was a barely perceptible figure shrouded in darkness. During the ensuing conversation, conducted through an interpreter who was himself barely visible, the visitor would be surprised to discover that his seated interlocutor was none other than Mehmed Ali Pasha himself. In numerous accounts visitors would comment on their inability to see clearly the Pasha's countenance, and they would consistently remark on how the chandeliers that were brought in "gave but little light".

The other theme that these travelers' accounts dwell on is the way Mehmed Ali, having lured and ensnared his visitors and piqued their curiosity, would suddenly reveal himself. At a crucial moment in the conversation he would lean forward dramatically to allow the candlelight to fall on his face. Alternatively, he would push back his turban from above his eyebrows giving the visitor a chance to catch his eye which until then had been thrown "into shade [and appeared to have] a sinister expression" (Scott, 1837, I, 178–179). In the final denouement of this subtle *coup de théâtre*, the European visitor, expecting with characteristic self-confidence to unravel this mysterious man, would be completely caught off his guard with the sudden realization that it was in fact *he* all along who had been scrutinized by the Pasha's piercing eyes. No wonder then that by the 1820s he had already become known as "one of the curiosities of Egypt" (Paton, 1863, II, 82–83).

We can now see how Mehmed Ali had so successfully contrived to wrap himself and his physical being in a cloak of mystery that exuded power and awe, and had succeeded in passing on to his numerous visitors the notion that his palaces, with their crowded entourage – and indeed Egypt as a whole – were centered in some essential way around his entire being and were watched over and commanded by his ever-present and vigilant eyes. Having only learned how to read and write after he had turned forty he would still remind his visitors that he was not in the habit of reading books. "The only books I read," he would warn them, "are men's faces, and I seldom read them amiss" (Murray, 1898, 4). Referring to Mehmed Ali's mesmerizing ability to see into and through people's souls and to intimidate not only his subjects but his visitors as well, the British Consul General, Henry Salt, wrote in 1817:

> Everything remains tranquil in Egypt … In fact everything now is set-tled [in the Citadel]. The Pashaw [sic] himself and the Kiya Bey [i.e. Mehmed Lazoğlu], a much devoted adherent, looking into every thing themselves with a scrupulous attention that baffles intrigue and render all opposition to their orders dangerous in the extreme. (British National Archives, 1817)

As much as Mehmed Ali might have wanted to instill in the minds of his officials and subjects alike the notion that he could be in more than one place at once, he was after all only human. To perpetuate his "presence" therefore, he was in the habit of dictating letters as soon as he took up position on his divan – called *al-Ma'iyya al-Saniyya*, or, lit-erally, the "Exalted Entourage". After meeting with his various visi-tors, reading through the various reports that his aides would forward to him, and addressing the many petitions that he received daily, he would then start dictating his responses to all the informa-tion that he had received. These *responsa* and memos which are now preserved in their thousands in the Egyptian National Archives (the *Ma'iyya* itself having been transformed into one of the most fre-quently consulted units within the Archives) bear all the hallmarks of the Pasha's character and it is easy to see how their fiery and intim-idating language was intended to propagate the Pasha's presence throughout his realm.

Given the elaborate ways he would manipulate situations to estab-lish his "presence", and the success with which he disseminated his power throughout Egypt, Mehmed Ali's words – whether written or spoken, even his very desires – literally became law. "So completely have [Egypt's] interests been identified with those of its ruler," wrote a British traveler in the 1830s, "that to speak of the government, commerce, policy, etc. of Egypt is to speak of the character of Mohammed Ali, who may justly apply to himself the noted words of an equally despotic potentate: '*L'Egypte, c'est moi*'" (Scott, 1837, 102–103).

5

EXPANDING HORIZONS

If Mehmed Ali's tenure as governor of Egypt had only lasted until 1821, this already sixteen-year-long reign would have been greater than that of any previous Ottoman governor; he would certainly have been remembered for the remarkable changes that he implemented, the influence of which was felt across the whole of Egyptian society, especially the unprecedented degree to which his control now affected the lives of the ordinary people throughout the country. In addition, Egypt's own position was greatly enhanced within the Ottoman Empire due to the unequivocal successes which had taken place in Arabia.

Yet Mehmed Ali was destined to live for some thirty more years and during the second phase of his career he introduced further changes into the economy, the administration, and society in general, that would make his already significant accomplishments fade into insignificance. For during this second phase the administration that the Pasha had established over the previous decade-and-a-half was further consolidated and its control was extended into areas where no previous Egyptian state had dared to venture. More and more aspects of the daily lives of Egyptians were being monitored, controlled and manipulated by this new administration. At the same time new institutions, schools, hospitals, factories, as well as an impressive army and a formidable navy – all tied to this new administration – radically altered the face of Egyptian society. Together they drastically transformed the relationship that the population had with its government. After the expansion of the

Pasha's influence eastward to Arabia during the 1810s, during the 1820s he expanded southward to the Sudan and north to the island of Crete, and Morea in southern Greece. And although no serious clash broke out between him and the sultan, it was becoming increasingly clear that a head-on confrontation was looming on the horizon.

A FORTUITOUS YEAR

Coming roughly midway through his long career, the year 1237 AH/1821–1822 CE was a significant one in Mehmed Ali's life – something that he himself realized. In an interview with the British Consul which he gave in 1827, he said, "I have now been twenty-two years Pasha – in the last six years [i.e., since 1821–1822] I have done more than in the preceding years … If I live but six or seven more years, I shall be able to mature my plans and affect something of consequence" (British National Archives, 1827a). The importance of 1821–1822 is due to two related developments which occurred during that year and which together would take Mehmed Ali's power to hitherto unprecedented heights. The first was the introduction of a particular brand of long-staple cotton (whose fibers were at least 1.75 inches/45 mm in length) and its cultivation on a large scale in the Delta. A French textile engineer by the name of Louis Alexis Jumel is usually credited with the widespread introduction of this brand of cotton. He had arrived in Egypt in 1817 and was employed by the Pasha as director of a projected spinning and weaving mill. After he had seen the bushes in the garden of Maho Bey (one of Mehmed Ali's acquaintances) he experimented with the new brand in his own garden throughout 1820. When the Pasha was informed of these experiments he encouraged Jumel's researches and forwarded 125,000 piastres to him and, following the success of the 1821 harvest, Mehmed Ali gave orders for the new cotton to be planted on a large scale. It eventually came to be known as Jumel (or Maho) cotton and it soon found voracious markets in Europe, especially in England where only the Lancashire mills with the latest machinery could handle the fineness of its quality. With the monopolies policy firmly in place, and with Mehmed Ali effectively acting as the sole merchant through whom European firms could import this coveted commodity, the Pasha's revenues grew exponentially, and in a good year the proceeds of cotton exportation contributed anything between one-third and one-quarter of his overall income.

As with other innovations introduced by Mehmed Ali, the social cost of introducing long-staple cotton was very high. In the past most of the areas cultivated had been devoted to winter crops with the land remaining idle during the summer months. However, with the introduction of long-staple cotton – spring-planted and fall-harvested – peasants had to labor throughout the year, and many women and children were also involved in the cultivation of the new crop, especially during harvest time. Peasants were also dragged into the corvée gangs whose work was needed to clear the existing irrigation canals and dig new ones. While there is some evidence that, shortly after the introduction of the Jumel cotton, peasants were paid a satisfactory price that made the extra effort worth their while, in the long run the new crop rotation policies of the Pasha were carried out through coercion. Harsh measures were stipulated for those who resisted the strict regulations that managed the cultivation of cotton. For example, those who dared to uproot their cotton plants were sentenced to life imprisonment and those who fled their villages to avoid cultivation labor, paying taxes, corvée or any of the many other government demands, were caught and sent back to their villages.

If the introduction of long-staple cotton was a fortuitous development that allowed the Pasha to increase his revenue to such a vast extent, albeit at a huge social cost, the second major development of 1821–1822 was the culmination of a prolonged process of trial and error which had gone into setting up a reliable military force – a consequence of the Pasha's deep-seated anxiety about his relationship with the Porte (the Ottoman government). This was achieved finally in February 1822 when Mehmed Ali arrived at the fateful decision to conscript Egyptians to serve in a new standing army, required above all to protect his realm and his nascent household government. After both previous attempts – firstly, to train the Albanian soldiers along European lines, and secondly, to capture Sudanese slaves – had failed, Mehmed Ali took a serious gamble by ordering the provincial governors in Upper Egypt to gather 4000 peasants and to send them to specially created training camps in Aswan. Initially it was decided that these peasants would be conscripted for a period of only three years, after which time they were to be given a stamped certificate proving that they had served in the army, and also to be given a life-long exemption from the land tax. In practice, however, these conscripts were often pressed into the army for life.

The training of these conscripts was entrusted to Mehmed Lazoğlu, the Pasha's faithful deputy who was now promoted to a new post, *cihadiye nazırı*, or "director of the army". Assisting him was a French officer by the name of Sève who claimed to have been a colonel in Napoleon's army and to have fought with the French emperor in Waterloo. Sève would later convert to Islam and assume the name Süleyman and be in charge of training all troops, soldiers and officers. In a characteristic Ottoman manner, Mehmed Ali decided to form the nucleus of the officer corps from among his for-mer white slaves, mostly Georgians and Circassians. Around 500 of his own slaves and 300 of his son's, Ibrahim Pasha, were trained by Süleyman Bey (later Pasha) in a special camp also in Aswan.

Mehmed Ali had clearly learned the lessons of earlier governors, most notably Hüsrev Pasha, whose attempts to train soldiers along European lines were frustrated when the new recruits resisted the harsh discipline, grumbled for their delayed pay and intermingled with the poor in the Cairo markets causing serious threats to urban security. To forestall such a possibility Mehmed Ali made sure that his new recruits were to be trained within tightly secured camps in the extreme south of the country and insisted that no intermingling between the new recruits and the wider society was to take place. At the same time, strict orders were issued to provincial governors to deliver enough food for these large numbers of men. Equally signifi-cant was the decision that the troops were to be clad in uniforms to be supplied by specially created workshops.

In short, what we are witnessing is the birth of a "modern" army, one that would be essentially different in three important aspects from any previous fighting force that the Pasha had had. The first was that this would be a standing army that would not dissipate after a particular campaign was over; the second was the fact that the soldiers of this intended army were prevented from securing their own food and would instead receive their pay, food and uniforms from the government; and thirdly, above all, the soldiers of this army were recruited from among the Arabic-speaking peasant population of Egypt, the first time in millennia that this had occurred.

In the space of ten years this army was to expand enormously, reaching the impressive figure of 130,000. Given a population of around five million, this meant that the army constituted 2.6 percent of the population – a very high percentage indeed. Although the creation of the army had a deep impact on the families of the conscripts, and on Egyptian rural society at large, what Egypt was to witness during this second phase of Mehmed Ali's long reign, and for which he is rightly famous, was a proliferation of all the many supporting institutions which were needed to maintain the army's existence. So it was actually the creation of the Pasha's army which was of overriding importance in the expansion of Egypt's administrative infrastructure, in that the many schools, hospitals and factories that were founded in Egypt during this period were established mainly to service this army. For the time being, though, and before it had time to prove its worth, the significance of this army lay in the enormous security dangers that its creation entailed. Mehmed Ali might have supposed that the conscription of Arabic-speaking peasants to be soldiers, rather than officers, in his intended army, while recruiting the officers from among members of his Turkish-speaking elite, might ease these security risks. He is reported to have once said, "I have done nothing in Egypt other than what the British are doing in India; they have an army composed of Indians and ruled by British officers, and I have an army composed of Arabs ruled by Turkish officers ... The Turk makes a better officer, since he knows that he is entitled to rule while the Arab feels that the Turk is better than him in that respect" (Douin, 1927, 110–111). This ethnic division of labor was intended to minimize the risks involved in gathering peasants from their villages and arming them, just as resentment against the Pasha's policies was reaching its peak. After sixteen years of Mehmed Ali's rule the Egyptian peasants were becoming increasingly frustrated at the Pasha's policies because they were seen to be exceedingly oppressive. The decision to drag them off into his army came after a series of measures in which they had found their physical labors were being used to further the Pasha's own goals. After heavy taxes on their lands, longer and more brutal corvée service on distant infrastructure projects, and a tight monopolies policy that prevented them from being able to consume the very products that they themselves had cultivated, conscription proved to be one step too many for the peasants to bear.

Immediately after conscription orders were sent to provincial governors in the Delta, a large uprising erupted there during April and May 1823, and peasants refused to pay taxes in many areas. Mehmed Ali dealt with this challenge in a characteristically prompt and decisive manner: he summoned his leading generals to a "war council" at his palace and, arming himself with six field cannons, he then marched on the villages himself. In less than a week the revolt was crushed.

A year later in April 1824 a larger rebellion was to erupt in Upper Egypt which soon engulfed all the villages and towns between Qus and Isna. Up to 30,000 men and women joined this new uprising which was led by a certain charismatic leader known as Shaykh Ahmed. He had revealed himself to be the long-awaited messianic *mahdi* and, declaring Mehmed Ali to be an infidel, he urged his followers to attack the Pasha's provincial officials. Reports of looting and arson on a large scale followed, and in numerous towns peasants marched on the residences of local officials, set fire to public buildings and, in some cases, took the Pasha's officials prisoner.

This was the most serious challenge to Mehmed Ali's authority so far, and dealing with it entailed a huge gamble. There was every likelihood that if the newly trained troops were sent to suppress the uprising that had erupted in the same villages from which conscripts had been recruited, this would carry with it the risk of the soldiers joining forces with the rebels and the peasant rebellion being transformed into an army mutiny. And sure enough, the Pasha's worst fears came to fruition as more than 700 newly conscripted soldiers joined the ranks of the rebels. Mehmed Ali, however, did not budge: he issued firm orders to the Turkish-speaking generals to deal with both the peasant rebels and the army mutineers ruthlessly. Receiving these orders, the new generals set aside military codes and *literally* decimated the mutinous units: soldiers were ordered to stand in line and every tenth man was shot. In addition, forty-five newly appointed officers were executed in front of their men. As for the villagers, the whole wrath of modern fighting armies was unleashed on them without mercy. In the ensuing fierce battles between peasants and soldiers more than 3000 villagers were killed. In a noteworthy incident a corporal was ordered to deal with people from his own village, and as bad luck would have it, he confronted his own father who had joined the rebels. Having failed to convince him to give himself up, the soldier shot and killed his father. The case was so remarkable that it was brought to the attention of Mehmed Ali in Cairo who issued an order promoting the corporal.

The brutality with which these mass uprisings were met made it clear to the peasants that open rebellion was not an option; however, they soon employed other more individual tactics to avoid serving in the Pasha's army. One was to try to leave their villages as soon as they heard of the impending visit of a conscription gang. Foreign visitors repeatedly commented on villages that were "buried in their stillness … where the dwellings of the poor inhabitants … still standing, neither blackened by fire, nor destroyed by war, but deprived of their inhabitants [who escaped the agents of the Pasha] by giving up house and home, and deserting *en masse*, the devoted town or village" (Madden, 1841, 41–42). The government attempted to control this phenomenon in the same way as it attempted to deal with those who dared to escape their villages to evade taxation, corvée or cotton cultivation labor: villagers had to carry permits to move from one village to another; villages as well as Bedouin shaykhs were ordered to be on the lookout for those passing through their lands; and those found to be harboring absconders were severely punished. Another tactic employed by the peasants was to desert their units after being conscripted. In spite of the hard beating that was meted out to deserters who were caught, desertion reached epidemic proportions: an investigation carried out in 1837 put the number of deserters in the army at 60,000, in addition to 20,000 deserters from the navy. Given that the size of the army at that time could not have exceeded 130,000, this meant that for every two conscripts, one soldier had managed to escape. Most tragically, there were those who attempted to evade serving in the army by maiming themselves in the hope that they would be deemed medically unfit for service. The most common techniques of self-maiming were putting rat poison in their eyes to induce temporary blindness; chopping off the index finger to be incapable of pulling the trigger and pulling the front teeth to be incapable of loading their muskets. Mehmed Ali met these tragic acts of defiance with characteristic determination: the self-maimed were not to avoid conscription and soon orders were issued to form entire battalions of the maimed and injured!

THE GREEK WAR

The ruthless tactics employed by the Pasha's agents in quelling rural uprisings, the uncompromising discipline that Mehmed Lazoğlu imposed on the new recruits, the strict training regime that had been set down by Süleyman Bey, and, above all, the unwavering determination of Mehmed Ali, succeeded in overcoming this dangerous resistance to the new conscription policy. The gamble of arming the peasants at a time of deep resentment against the Pasha and his policies seems to have paid off. Furthermore, the decision to assign officers who were ethnically and linguistically different from the men they commanded was instrumental in creating a well-trained and dependable fighting machine. Following his success in subduing the first wave of rural uprisings in 1823–1824, the Pasha dropped his hesitation about the speed with which conscription should go ahead, a hesitation that was based, among other things, on fears that conscription might affect agricultural production by taking away greatly needed manpower. Orders were henceforth issued to his provincial governors to gather as many able-bodied men as could be found in the countryside.

No sooner had these troops finished their initial training and been put to the test in quelling these early uprisings than the Pasha received orders from Istanbul to send them to a new and dangerous destination. In March 1821 the Greek subjects of the Ottoman sultan had risen up in a large revolt that aimed at nothing less than complete independence from the Ottoman Empire. This.came at a particularly bad time for Sultan Mahmud as he had diverted a large number of his troops to fight the Persians on his eastern borders. Moreover, the young energetic sultan who, since his accession in 1808, had managed to subdue local notables and had tightened Istanbul's grip over the provinces, found himself forced to reverse his policy by turning to Mehmed Ali to help him suppress the rebellion. Just as his predecessor, Sultan Selim III, had done fifteen years earlier, Mahmud found himself trapped between a rock and a hard place as he knew that the means he deployed to pacify one province could very well lead to strengthening the governor of another.

On his part, Mehmed Ali, feeling more and more secure in his province and confident about his newly trained troops, did not hesitate for long in answering his sovereign's demand. Seeing that the *firman* he received from Istanbul entailed appointing his son, Ibrahim Pasha, as governor of Morea (i.e., the Peloponnese, the southern peninsula of the Greek mainland), he seized the opportunity to use his disciplined and tested army to further his reputation within the empire. In July 1824 after a six-month preparation period during which time the Pasha managed to put together a large fleet, the new army, which had by then reached the figure of 17,000 infantry troops in addition to 700 cavalrymen, left under the command of Ibrahim Pasha. After some months of being chased by Greek fire ships that restricted his movements, Ibrahim finally managed to land on the Greek mainland in February 1825. He immediately deployed his troops in open field against the Greeks and in repeated military confrontations he inflicted heavy defeats on them. Soon he had captured one city after another until Athens itself fell on 5 June 1827. It was becoming clear that Mehmed Ali's new army had been successful beyond all expectations and that behind these victories on the battlefield lay the professional training that the troops had received while in Egypt, along with Ibrahim's talents as a military commander and Mehmed Ali's mastery of managerial and logistical details that guaranteed that the army was kept well supplied, well fed and well clothed.

Yet, and in spite of these spectacular successes, Mehmed Ali had many reasons to worry about the conduct of the war in the Peloponnese. For one thing, maintaining such a large number of troops entailed a very heavy burden on his finances especially given the very low Nile in 1825 and the failure of the harvest of that year and of the next. In addition, the continued demand for men for the army was responsible for the below-average cotton harvest of these two years, putting further pressure on his finances.

THE INVOLVEMENT OF THE EUROPEAN POWERS

The increasing involvement of the European powers in the Greek conflict was another source of anxiety. At the start of the conflict these powers were not much concerned with the cause of the Greek rebels, but when it became clear that the sultan was incapable of dealing with them swiftly, the European powers' position began to change. The Russian tsar, although not much enthused by the Greek revolutionary ideals, gradually became increasingly sympathetic to their cause. The other European powers – namely Britain, France and Austria – were anxious lest the conflict escalate into a Russo–Ottoman war because they feared that the inevitable result of such a war would be an Ottoman defeat and the southward expansion of Russia at the expense of the Ottomans. Over time, though, the British shifted their position as they now saw that it was in their best interest to ally themselves with the Russians and put pressure on the Ottomans to grant the Greeks limited autonomy under the sultan's suzerainty.

Gradually, Mehmed Ali became aware of these European diplomatic moves and as soon as he got involved in the Greek war he found himself being called upon in his palace in Alexandria by countless European statesmen. With typical shrewdness he managed to allay many of their fears and expressed his desire for a speedy resolution of the conflict. Reading the numerous accounts left behind by the Pasha's visitors during these tense months, one sees the Pasha gloating in the limelight of international affairs. However, he also realized that what he had got himself into was no longer an internal Ottoman affair, for what the Sublime Porte (as the Ottoman government was then called) was seeing as an internal insubordination by the sultan's Greek subjects, was being judged in Europe as a national war of independence in which a Christian subject people were rising against their Turkish oppressors. The Pasha's European visitors were indicating that a shift in European public opinion was perceptible and that military action in support of the Greek rebels could not be ruled out. Given Mehmed Ali's extensive commercial dealings with Europe, especially Britain and France, a military confrontation with Europe was something he neither desired nor could afford.

HÜSREV'S REAPPEARANCE

Above all, Mehmed Ali was alarmed to find that his old enemy, Hüsrev Pasha, was also deeply involved in the fight against the Greek insurgents. Ever since his departure from Egypt, Hüsrev had been appointed to one senior position after another. As governor of Bosnia in 1806 he succeeded in pacifying the Serbian revolt of that year. He was also entrusted to deal with a Kurdish uprising in his capacity as governor of Erzurum in eastern Anatolia in 1818. After the outbreak of the Greek rebellion the sultan appointed him in the prestigious position of grand admiral of the Ottoman navy (December 1822) and orders were issued to him and to Mehmed Ali to cooperate together. Not unexpectedly, Mehmed Ali was adamant that he could not work with his old enemy and he sent numerous letters to Istanbul complaining of Hüsrev's behavior and insisting on his dismissal from the joint command of the combined Ottoman–Egyptian navy and that his son be given a free hand in running military operations.

Finally, and when all his pleas to remove Hüsrev went unheeded, Mehmed Ali resorted to threats. Realizing how important he had become within the empire and how dependent the sultan was on him, he sent a letter to Istanbul saying that if Hüsrev was not dismissed from the command of the navy, he would ask his son to cease his efforts against the Greek rebels. Two weeks later the Porte acquiesced and dismissed Hüsrev from his post adding yet another score for Mehmed Ali against his old rival. However, before he had enough time to enjoy this small victory against Hüsrev, Mehmed Ali received news that Hüsrev had been appointed in May 1827 to yet another important, and dangerous, new position, namely, as *serasker*, or commander-in-chief, of a new army that Sultan Mahmud had created.

THE "AUSPICIOUS EVENT"

On the night of 14 June 1826 after the Janissaries, the age-old troops of the Ottoman Empire, figured out that Sultan Mahmud had been plotting to reform the army and that the reforms were bound to affect them adversely, they overturned their cauldrons in a typical gesture indicating that they were staging a mutiny. Nineteen years earlier the Janissaries had revolted against Sultan Selim III when he attempted a similar reform, and as has been mentioned above, they ended up deposing Selim and then killing him, thus stopping the reform program in its tracks. This time, however, it was clear that Mahmud had learnt from his predecessor's mistakes. It is also very plausible that he was inspired by Mehmed Ali's successful elimination of the Mamluks in 1811 and that he had to perform a massacre of the rebel leaders if need be. For no sooner had the Janissaries announced their mutiny than they were encircled in their barracks and orders given to loyal artillery battalions to fire on the mutineers. Soon the entire barracks was set on fire and those who managed to escape were killed on the spot. In what came to be known as the *Vaka-i Hayriye*, or Auspicious Event, around 6000 Janissaries were slaughtered. In this event the Ottoman sultan did what his strong governor in Egypt had managed to do fifteen years earlier, and in one fell swoop his army's old guard which stood against all attempts at reform was wiped out.

Mehmed Ali received this news with alarm given that the sultan was now free to rebuild his armed forces, with all the risks that this entailed to his own position in Egypt. Finding out that his old enemy, Hüsrev, was appointed as commander-in-chief of the new army must have been unwelcome news. Shortly afterwards, when the grand vizier sent a request to him for officers from his army to train the new Ottoman soldiers because of the successes that Mehmed Ali's troops were exhibiting on the Greek battlefields, the Pasha wasted no time in turning down the request using unconvincing pretexts.

DISASTER AT NAVARINO

Meanwhile dark clouds were gathering over the army in Greece. A joint French–British–Russian fleet was roaming the waters of the Aegean and Mehmed Ali took this as a very ominous sign. For months he had been writing to Istanbul warning against the changing tide of European public opinion and urging the Porte to resolve the Greek crisis by negotiation, even if this meant granting the Greeks some kind of autonomous status within the empire. But Istanbul was adamant in its insistence that the Greek insurgency was to be crushed by force, and strict orders were passed to Ibrahim to spare no village if it was proved to be backing the insurgents. In desperation, Mehmed Ali wrote to his agent in Istanbul telling him that he and the

Europeans were on a collision course. He added that he could not bear the responsibility for the death of thousands of Muslims which, he argued, would be the inevitable result of a naval confrontation with the European navies. He pleaded with his agent to intercede with the Porte to accept a compromise. Istanbul, however, did not budge, and on 20 October 1827 disaster struck as heavily as Mehmed Ali had predicted. In a matter of a few hours the European navies trapped the combined Egyptian–Ottoman navy in the Bay of Navarino, and after the battle was over, the entire Egyptian–Ottoman navy was destroyed, its ships either sunk or burnt.

This was a severe blow to Mehmed Ali as he was now left without a fleet to protect his dominions. He was convinced that this heavy loss was not caused by any oversight on his part, nor was it the result of any negligence by his son, Ibrahim. Rather, he was adamant that the disaster at Navarino was a direct result of the Porte's intransigence and, specifically, of Hüsrev's incompetent interference – an opinion shared by many in the Ottoman capital. Mehmed Ali was therefore keen to cut his losses and refused to listen to the Porte's requests to continue the fight against the Greek rebels. Instead he opened negotiations directly with the Europeans which would guarantee his son's withdrawal from the Greek mainland.

The Greek debacle proved to be a turning point in Mehmed Ali's relationship with Istanbul, for it showed him not only how influential he had become within the Ottoman Empire but also how costly his assistance to the sultan was to him. Although the idea of complete independence had still not been contemplated, the need to keep his distance from the Porte's policies was becoming ever more pressing. So when Istanbul asked again for his assistance in its war against the Russians (a war that eventually led to the declaration of complete Greek independence), Mehmed Ali sent Istanbul a resounding rejection.

In letters to his son Mehmed Ali blamed his old enemy, Hüsrev, for his own precarious position within the empire. Yet, he also knew that his own tensions with the Porte far exceeded this personal rivalry with Hüsrev. Mehmed Ali was aware that his policies in Egypt which allowed him to transform Cairo into a rival center of military, economic and diplomatic power within the empire were essentially contradicting Sultan Mahmud's ardent attempts at centralization and reform. Furthermore, Sultan Mahmud's calling upon Mehmed Ali to assist him in his wars against the Wahhabi and Greek rebels was part of the sultan's larger design to curtail regional autonomy and to extend the central authority of his government throughout his realm. From 1814 to 1820 Mahmud had managed to eliminate local dynasties in Thrace, Macedonia, the Danubian shores and much of Wallachia (in present-day Romania). Moreover, the Anatolian notables had suffered a similar fate to their counterparts in the Balkans. And then, closest to home was Ali Pasha of Yanina, who had established a powerbase in Albania and had formed a small army of his own. Soon, however, he was besieged in his castle by Ottoman troops and had his head cut off and sent to Istanbul to be displayed outside the sultan's palace (February 1822). There were therefore many precedents of local dynasts who were severely punished for their independent stance and, as confident as Mehmed Ali might have felt about his increased security within Egypt, there were certainly enough reasons to be anxious about the future.

PREPARATION FOR THE NEXT ROUND

In characteristically strident fashion, Mehmed Ali did not sit around waiting for Istanbul to strike first. Immediately after the Greek debacle he set about rebuilding his lost fleet. He decided not to buy ships from Europe as he had done before but, remarkably, to construct a fleet in Egypt. He therefore hired a French naval engineer, M. de Cerisy, and entrusted him with the enormous task of building an arsenal in Alexandria. In the space of four years the first of the new ships – a 100-gun ship bearing the Pasha's name – was launched and was soon followed by numerous other warships. This was not the first time the Pasha had tried to build ships himself. As early as 1809, in anticipation of the Arabian campaign, he had issued orders for his

workmen to construct a small arsenal in Bulaq, Cairo's river port, and
for the pieces to be carried on camel-back and then assembled in Suez.
Yet the scale of the Alexandria dockyard – by the mid-1830s it had
more than 8000 laborers – and the fact that many of the laborers who
toiled there were either convicted criminals or peasants serving their
corvée duty, dwarfs earlier attempts by the Pasha to build a naval force.

Preparations for a possible military confrontation with the Porte
were not limited to building naval installations though and, during
the second half of the 1820s, fervent activities were witnessed
throughout Egypt aimed at enhancing the Pasha's military and
financial capabilities. For example, the Pasha issued orders to the
director of the arsenal he had established in 1815–1816 in the Cairo
Citadel to increase the production of cannons, swords and muni-
tions. By the mid 1820s it is said that this arsenal was producing muskets at the rate of 1600 a month. Mehmed Ali also took the decision
that much of his new army's uniforms, footwear and headgear would
be supplied domestically rather than from abroad. In 1825, therefore, a fez factory was founded and it soon managed to produce
24,000 hats a month. Monopolizing the cotton crop and encouraged
by the conversion of a silk factory, founded in 1816, to cotton spinning, the Pasha gave orders for the construction of thirty textile factories. These factories employed between 12,000 and 15,000
laborers in the 1820s and, with the exception of a few imported
machines, most of the equipment used in them was produced by
Egyptian craftsmen. The spinning jennies used in these factories
(estimated to be around 1380 jennies) were turned by animals; three
factories, however, had steam engines that had been imported from
England.

Most impressive of all the measures taken to enhance the Pasha's
fighting capacity was the establishment in 1827 of a large training
hospital in Abu Za'bal to the northeast of Cairo. Given the huge cost
in lives paid by the slaves who were rounded up during the Sudan
campaign, Mehmed Ali realized the necessity to create a medical
corps that could treat the men conscripted to the army. This was a
hard lesson to be learned and one that was repeated in the Greek

campaign where it transpired that the number of the soldiers who died of disease and untreated wounds exceeded those who had died in actual combat. Furthermore, the haphazard way in which the conscription orders were conducted without any medical screening resulted in gathering thousands of men who were later proven to be unfit for military service.

All these factors, as well as the validity of the arguments presented by Dr Antoine Barthélemy Clot who was hired in 1825 as chief of the military medical corps, convinced the Pasha that his fighting force had to be protected by a professional medical corps and that it would be cheaper and more efficient if doctors could be trained at home rather than seeking the services of foreign doctors. Crucially Clot insisted that in order for these new doctors to be able to communicate with their patients, the proposed medical school should use Arabic (as opposed to French or Turkish) as its language of instruction. Clot also urged that medical instruction should be based on anatomical medicine and that students should learn pathology by dissecting human cadavers. Mehmed Ali accepted the advice of this Frenchman, who later came to be known as Clot Bey, and in due course the Qasr al-'Aini training hospital was founded in 1827 and grew to become a complex medical center whose impact in the long run expanded beyond the confines of the army to include healthcare facilities for the larger civilian population as well.

Besides medical services, the new army also created the need for many other skills which called for the foundation of various specialized schools and polytechnics. While most of these educational institutions were opened in the 1830s, it is important to note that Mehmed Ali's interest in education predated the founding of his army in 1821–1822. Soon after getting rid of the Mamluk leaders in 1811, Mehmed Ali became the owner of many young Mamluks whose masters had died in the massacre and in a typical Ottoman fashion he proceeded to provide them with military training in a special school he established in the Citadel. In 1815 in his own palace in Shubra he also opened another school to teach engineering and land surveying to young Egyptians; known as the "School of

Engineering", students were taught arithmetic, geometry, trigonometry and algebra.

However, the creation of the new army marked a qualitative change in the Pasha's interest in education. As mentioned, the training of the new cadets and soldiers required opening two special schools in the south of the country. Realizing the importance of these schools, Mehmed Ali appointed his own deputy as director of one of them and the Frenchman Colonel Sève (Süleyman Pasha) as director of the second one. In 1825 a large school was opened in Cairo to prepare students for advanced technical training in various fields, i.e. infantry, artillery and cavalry. The first intake of this technical school was approximately 500 students, composed mainly of Circassians, Albanians, Greeks and Armenians.

The full implications of the Pasha's educational, medical and industrial policies were not felt until the late 1830s and beyond. Towards the end of the 1820s however Mehmed Ali was still experimenting with different and innovative ideas on how to increase his revenue and to lodge himself ever more securely in Egypt, and following the serious setback of Navarino it did not take him much time to get back on his feet. Indeed, in just a few years he had not only managed to recover his losses but had considerably increased his fighting capabilities with the foundation of a new navy, by the expansion of his army with fresh conscripts, and by supplementing their effectiveness with medical, educational and industrial establishments.

By 1830 it appeared that Mehmed Ali was in a position to withstand virtually any attempt by the Porte to remove him from his coveted post; indeed, he was now ready to seize the initiative and to launch a pre-emptive strike on the Sultan's dominions in Syria.

6

THE FINAL SHOWDOWN

The 1830s marked a clear departure in Mehmed Ali's career whereby he found himself at the center not only of Ottoman affairs, but also of world politics. During this decade his military activities triggered what came to be known as the Egyptian question – a diplomatic crisis that was to transform Egypt's international position; the inauguration of unprecedented reforms within the Ottoman Empire, known as the *Tanzimat*, was necessary, thus altering the relationship that the Empire had with European powers and deeply affecting internal European politics. Above all, the Egyptian question was only to be resolved when the Pasha had finally succeeded in extracting from the Ottoman sultan a precious *firman* that secured his position in Egypt definitively. Given that soon after his arrival in Egypt when he was in his early thirties he had managed to transform himself from a mere village bully into a fledgling politician, his transition into the role of an international statesman in the 1830s when he was then in his sixties was a further impressive reinvention of himself.

THE BENEFACTOR

Throughout the 1820s, as we have seen, the Pasha managed to strengthen his control over Egypt, at the same time as reinforcing his household rule. His relatives and friends were now occupying key positions either as heads of these new institutions, which had been brought into existence by the establishment of the army, or as provincial governors. Seeing him literally as *veli nimet* (Ar. *waliyy al-ni'am*), or the Benefactor, many members of this new elite tied their future to his well-being. He also managed to include in his larger elite those hundreds of students who entered his educational institutions, or those few among them who were chosen to travel to Europe for advanced studies. Remarkably, his old rival Hüsrev Pasha, a freedman with no children of his own, had embarked on a similar path of increasing his household in Istanbul by adopting an exceptionally large number of boys, paying for their education in the state's new schools and, on their graduation, pushing for their employment in key positions in the bureaucracy. Mehmed Ali's "household government", therefore, was not peculiar to him; rather, it was a common feature of Ottoman politics at that time. However, by the late 1820s Mehmed Ali could feel confident that his domestic powerbase was as strong as any other within the far-flung Ottoman Empire and that he had a dependable elite around him – one that acted at his bidding, albeit not always with the efficiency he demanded.

Indeed, the increased sense of security he felt in Egypt was also reflected in the patriarchal language he deployed in referring to his subjects at large. In a circular issued in 1828 it was stated that "the *waliyy al-ni'am* ... aims at bestowing his attention and care on all who reside in Egyptian lands and to consider them as if they were his own private estate. He strives to raise in his bounty all the residents of Egypt, young and old, high-ranking or commoner, and to treat them as his own children" (*Al-Waqa'i' al-Misriyya*, 1829). In a meeting he had with the British consul general in 1827 he said that he derived "pleasure in considering [his subjects] as his own children. He confessed that he had oppressed them ... till within the last two years but that since that time he had behaved to them as a father" (British National Archives, 1827b). And in an interview with a French traveler he said of the Egyptians: "This people has to be led as children, for if we leave them to their own devices they will return to the state of disorder from which I had elevated them" (Douin, 1927, 99).

NAGGING WORRIES

Despite the increasing sense of security that he was feeling domestically, Mehmed Ali nevertheless had reasons to be anxious about his future. For one thing, he was not getting any younger and the death of those closest to him (his beloved wife, Emine, died in 1824, and his trusted deputy, Lazoğlu, in 1827) must have poignantly reminded him of his own mortality. At the same time the ambivalent relationship he had with Istanbul was a source of constant concern and, as he told the British consul, the more he invested his effort domestically by building institutions, inaugurating reforms and cementing his powerbase, the more he wondered who would benefit from all his efforts after his own death (Kutluoğlu, 1998, 126).

Furthermore, news arriving from Necib Efendi, his agent in the Ottoman capital, indicated that Istanbul was gradually adopting a belligerent stance. The sprightly efforts of Sultan Mahmud to tighten his grip over the provinces – the abolition of the old Janissary corps that led the way to reforming the sultan's military forces, and the rapid measures taken to revitalize the empire's bureaucracy and to revamp its finances – were all alarming signs that the Ottoman center was rapidly centralizing its control, and that the semi-independent policies adopted by governors like Mehmed Ali would no longer be tolerated. Above all, it was clear from reports he received from Istanbul that his old enemy, Hüsrev Pasha, was assuming more and more power there and had the ear of the sultan.

At the same time, developments in Europe were equally alarming. News was filtering through to the Pasha from several sources – the commercial agents he sent to various Mediterranean ports, the European travelers whom he took pleasure in granting an audience, the European ambassadors in Istanbul about whom his agent there was sending detailed reports, and, above all, the consuls representing the various European powers in Cairo and Alexandria – they all told him that some European capitals were starting to raise serious doubts about the actual viability of the age-old Ottoman state. Although it had been clear for a long time that the European powers were increasingly gaining the upper hand in military confrontations with the Ottoman Empire, Mehmed Ali's experience in the Greek war showed him how Europe was now interfering in domestic affairs within the empire, and had successfully carved a new state out of the sultan's dominions.

With piecemeal news coming in and a lack of ambassadors within the European capitals, it must have been difficult for Mehmed Ali to figure out what plans were being hatched. He did his best to compensate for this handicap by employing his many and well-practised skills of charm and eloquence on the European consuls, milking whatever information he could out of them while at the same time manipulating them to convey his thoughts and wishes back to their superiors.

It was during one of these numerous meetings with European consuls that he received a bizarre offer which indicated that changes on a grand scale were being contemplated in European capitals. During a meeting in 1828 with the French consul, Drovetti, he was informed that Paris was interested in seeking his assistance in an invasion of Algeria, nominally an Ottoman province. In the ensuing negotiations Mehmed Ali demanded four men-o'-war ships and ten million francs, to which the French were only too eager to agree. Soon however the Pasha got wind of strong British and Russian opposition to the plan, and this, together with his realization that his interests lay elsewhere, made him turn down the offer and the whole project was dropped. This curious Algerian interlude must have given him an indication, though, of the scale of these European plans to gnaw away at Ottoman possessions.

THE INVASION OF SYRIA

As alarming as the British and Russian opposition to his participation in the French Algerian plan was, the main reason why Mehmed Ali let go of the idea was that an invasion of Algeria would divert him from defending his northern frontier. It was in Syria and not Algeria that Mehmed Ali's strategic interests lay. The Pasha's sights had been focused on Syria since his very early years as governor of Egypt: Syria was rich with forests that could supply him with the much-needed timber for his fleet. Its population, albeit smaller than that of Egypt, could offset the shortage of manpower caused by his conscription and demanding infrastructure policies. Above all, Mehmed Ali's interest in Syria was calculated, and related to his continuing sense of insecurity about Istanbul's next move. Any attempt by the Porte to pluck him out of Egypt by force would logically be made by launching an attack from there. Having therefore strengthened his naval power, beefed up Alexandria's defenses and constructed fortifications along the Mediterranean coast, what remained necessary now was to protect the land frontier between the heartland of the Ottoman Empire and Syria.

Throughout the years of 1830–1831 speculations abounded about the real purpose of the fervent military activity that had been witnessed throughout Egypt. Some said that the Pasha was about to send further troops to Arabia while others surmised that he was complying with the Porte's orders to help with the war against Russia. During the summer of 1831 in particular unprecedented military preparations were noticed and, following a devastating cholera epidemic that left the army camps and barracks relatively untouched (thanks to the efforts of Dr Clot who was subsequently rewarded with the honorific title of "Bey"), the real intentions of the Pasha were finally revealed. They were nothing less than a full land and sea invasion of the Syrian provinces.

On 2 November 1831 the full power of the Pasha's new army was unleashed onto Syria. Using the pretext of the governor of Sidon in southern Palestine, Abdallah Pasha, giving refuge to some 6000 Egyptian peasants who had escaped the Pasha's draconian policies and who refused to hand them back, Mehmed Ali gave orders for two forces, a sea and a land one, to move to Acre. Within the space of one month Ibrahim's troops had already reached the city and laid siege on it.

The Porte responded by ordering Mehmed Pasha, the governor of Aleppo, to raise troops from the neighboring areas and to confront

Ibrahim Pasha's army. Fresh orders were also issued to Hüseyin Pasha, who had wiped out the Janissaries, to muster another force in Anatolia and to reconnoiter with Mehmed Pasha. In May 1832 a *fetva* was issued by the *ulama* of Anatolia declaring both Mehmed Ali and his son Ibrahim to be rebels.

None of these moves, however, managed to intimidate Mehmed Ali. The siege of Acre, moreover, despite dragging on for weeks and months, only strengthened his resolve. In an interview with a British traveler the Pasha predicted: "In a few days Acre will be mine. If the Sultan consent that I shall keep it, I will stop there; if not, I will take Damascus. There again, if Damascus be granted me, I will stop; but if not, I will take Aleppo; and if the Sultan will not then consent – who knows? Allah Kerim! – God is merciful" (St. John, 1834, II, 486). Uttered at a time when his son's troops had not yet captured Acre, and when public opinion in Syria was divided about the legality of his military move against the sultan, and with a *fetva* declaring him to be a rebel hanging over him, these words are a remarkable demonstration of Mehmed Ali's steadfastness and unflinching will-power. They also proved to be quite prophetic: on 27 May 1832 Acre finally fell, allowing Ibrahim to march on to Damascus and to enter it, without fighting, on 16 June. Three weeks later he encountered the vanguard of the Ottoman army and inflicted a heavy defeat on it. Soon thereafter Aleppo, the northernmost city in Syria, fell to Ibrahim Pasha.

CROSSING THE RUBICON

Within seven months of the army's departure from Egypt the entire Syrian provinces were under the command of Ibrahim Pasha. Some six months earlier in his interview with J. A. St. John, Mehmed Ali was unable to articulate what he would do in case Aleppo fell to his son; now that it had, he was still unclear about his next move. With military logic dictating events from day to day, matters on the ground continued to develop and for the following ten months it was clear that Mehmed Ali's mind was lagging behind his son's military victories.

In spite of capturing Aleppo, the main Ottoman army which had been gathered under Hüseyin Pasha had not been drawn into the confrontation. On 29 July Ibrahim Pasha crossed the Taurus Mountains and engaged Hüseyin Pasha's army, inflicting a heavy defeat on it. This was a very serious escalation of the conflict as Ibrahim had now crossed into Anatolia, the heartland of the Ottoman Empire. What made matters even more serious was that Ibrahim Pasha, building on the momentum of his army, was marching northward to engage with yet another army that Sultan Mahmud had raised and which had at its command Mehmed Reşid Pasha, the grand vizier. In December 1832 when the two armies clashed in Konya in central Anatolia the Ottomans were defeated yet again and Ibrahim even managed to capture the grand vizier himself.

This was the most significant military victory that Ibrahim had hitherto accomplished and with it the last fighting force that the Ottoman sultan had gathered was wiped out. The road to Istanbul was now wide open. Emissaries hurried between Mehmed Ali in Egypt and his son in Anatolia worried about the imminent collapse of the Ottoman Empire. However, the fascinating correspondence between father and son reveals an intriguing conundrum: neither man appeared to know how to invest this significant victory. Having launched what seemed to be a defensive pre-emptive strike aimed at capturing Acre and thus securing his northern borders, Mehmed Ali found his son sweeping not only through all of Syria but also advancing onward into Anatolia. The final victory at Konya surpassed his wildest expectations, and his political calculations raced to keep up with his son's territorial acquisitions.

After capturing the grand vizier of the Ottoman Empire and obliterating all the armies that had been amassed to stop his son's advance, Mehmed Ali had to think quickly about the terms of peace he could dictate on his now vanquished enemy. Soon the proposition of deposing the sultan and installing his son became explicit in the correspondence between Mehmed Ali and Ibrahim. With the army resuming its march on to the Ottoman capital, this idea acquired further shape: the *ulama* of Anatolia and Rumelia (that is, the Balkans) would be

prevailed upon to issue a *fetva* declaring Sultan Mahmud to have devi-
ated from the Faith and to ask for his dethronement. A pledge to protect the lives of the members of the ruling family was also suggested.

The flurry of diplomatic activity that followed Ibrahim's alarming
victories, however, induced the Pasha to seek a more moderate
stance. To begin with he got wind, from his son, of a request by the
sultan for British naval assistance which brought about further escalation when the British turned down the Ottoman request. This
prompted Sultan Mahmud to approach the Russians. Seeing this as a
golden opportunity to enhance their influence in the Ottoman capital, the Russians, having emerged from war with the sultan only five
years earlier, were all too willing to respond favorably. A Russian
envoy, General Muravieff, was sent on a special mission to both
Istanbul and Alexandria. Muravieff offered the sultan the promise of
Russian troops and warships and, in a meeting with Mehmed Ali in
Alexandria on 13 January 1833, he warned the Pasha that Russia
would not tolerate the dismemberment of the Ottoman Empire and
that the Pasha should order his son to halt his advance on the capital.
Given that the struggle between Mehmed Ali and the sultan had now
been transformed into a European crisis, and that all the leading
European capitals were now involved, he issued orders to his son to
stop his advance on Istanbul.

During the next three months Mehmed Ali found himself falling
under two contradictory influences: on the one hand, he was being
pressured by Istanbul and the European powers to withdraw his
troops and to reassert his subservience to the sultan; while on the
other, his son was encouraging him on to march on the capital and
"finish off the business". Mehmed Ali's mettle as a clever politician
manifested itself in his ability to handle these contradictory influences. He accepted his son's assessment of the military situation and
his pleas not to be "the first to blink". However, he also realized that
approving Ibrahim's impassioned plans to march on the capital or to
declare his complete independence would surely come up against the
wall of European objection. In other words, while he fully grasped
the extent of his own military strength, he also realized that he could

not translate the maximalist territorial expansions that his son was promising him into permanent diplomatic realities.

The resolution of what came to be known as the "first Syrian crisis" was couched in the "Convention of Kütahiya", named after the town where the negotiations were conducted, and which formed Ibrahim Pasha's furthermost expansion. According to this "Convention" the sultan re-bestowed the provinces of Egypt, Crete and the Hijaz on Mehmed Ali and his son, and granted Ibrahim Pasha the four Syrian provinces as well as the post of *muhassil*, or collector of taxes, of the strategic province of Adana in southern Anatolia – which was rich in timber and which held the key to an invasion of Anatolia from the south. When news arrived of the settlement "the Pasha [in the words of the British agent, Campbell] started up with tears of joy in his eyes, and laying aside anything like Turkish gravity, burst into a sort of hysteric laugh" (al-Sayyid Marsot, 1984, 230). His military adventure had been successful beyond all expectations and by entrusting the conduct of military operations to his son he managed to secure his northern borders. Furthermore, by grasping the full implications of his moves on European politics Mehmed Ali proved himself not only to be a first rate Ottoman politician but also a clever strategist who could think beyond the confines of the Ottoman world, as complex as these were, and factor in the intricacies of European politics.

REORGANIZATION AND RETRENCHMENT

In spite of his victories in this first round of military confrontations with the Ottoman sultan Mehmed Ali paradoxically found himself in a precarious situation. The fact that the "Convention of Kütahiya" was not an official peace treaty but only a verbal agreement between his son and the sultan's emissary meant that he had not secured a formal diplomatic agreement. Furthermore, as a direct result of his military action the Ottomans agreed to sign a defensive pact with Russia. This treaty weakened Mehmed Ali diplomatically as now both Britain and

France blamed him for offering the Russians the opportunity to increase their influence in Istanbul.

In an attempt to strengthen his hand Mehmed Ali went on the diplomatic offensive and officially announced to the European consuls his intention to declare himself independent from the Porte. This mention of independence was quickly rebuffed by all European powers and Mehmed Ali promptly shelved his talk of independence and gave the consuls firm pledges that he would preserve the status quo. These were not empty words, though, for he had every reason to catch his breath, so to speak, and to take stock of his military situation.

In addition to the standoff with the Ottomans Mehmed Ali was facing serious problems as to how to administer the large areas now under his control. Crete, which Sultan Mahmud had bestowed on him in recompense for his assistance in the Greek war, rose in a large revolt against the conscription policy that was extended there. At first, Mehmed Ali sent Osman Nureddin, the commander-in-chief of his navy, to deal with the uprising. Osman, however, declared a general amnesty to the rebels without first consulting with Mehmed Ali and then, fearing his master's wrath, he preferred to defect to Istanbul, never to return to Egypt. Mehmed Ali therefore felt obliged to go to Crete in person (July–September 1833) to deal with the rebels and to pacify the island.

Moreover, in Hijaz, Yemen and Sudan the Pasha's agents were facing serious administrative and military problems, many of which were caused by local opposition as well as by the lack of experience of the Pasha's civilian governors and military commanders. But it was in the newly conquered Syrian territories that the Pasha faced the strongest opposition. In spite of having a large army (around 50,000 troops that increased to some 100,000 men in the late 1830s) under the command of Ibrahim Pasha, and assisted by Süleyman Pasha; and in spite of appointing the experienced Mehmed Şerif Pasha, the Pasha's nephew, as governor-general of Syria, Mehmed Ali never managed to raise enough revenue from Syria to cover the cost of the occupation. Furthermore, his monopolies policy that had been extended to Syria faced stern opposition from the Europeans, and especially from the British, so he was finally forced to withdraw it. More seriously, the Syrians could not stomach the conscription and disarmament policies that Ibrahim attempted to impose on them. Large uprisings erupted – first in Palestine, then among the Druzes in Mount Lebanon, and finally in Beirut – and Mehmed Ali felt the need to go to Syria during the first of these uprisings (March–July 1834) to help his son restore law and order, something that was eventually achieved with extreme ruthlessness.

Domestically, Mehmed Ali was faced with an increasingly resentful population. There was a disgruntled elite clamoring to have more of a say in how to run the country, combined with a tightening economic situation made more difficult by the rising cost of his medical, industrial and educational enterprises. Above all there was the very heavy financial burden of his armies in the Sudan, Yemen, the Hijaz, Crete and Syria. To combat these difficulties he ordered a complete overhaul of his expanding administration and issued a law in 1837 creating seven *divan*s (departments) to manage, respectively, the internal affairs of state, finances, the army, the navy, education, foreign trade and factories. However, these new departments were not given any significant degree of independence and their decisions still had to be approved by him in person.

The first half of the 1830s saw the Pasha's revenues significantly reduced: first of all, a cholera epidemic in 1831–1832 killed 120,000 people, and was followed by a series of low floods which led to serious famine in the countryside, together with a devastating plague epidemic in 1834–1835 which killed a further 200,000 people. All these disasters affected the country's manpower and reduced its productivity. A sudden fall in cotton prices caused by the international business crisis of 1836–1837 exacerbated an already difficult financial situation, forcing some serious measures to be taken. First to be affected was the educational sector: out of sixty-seven primary schools that had been opened in 1833, twenty-three were closed down. Soon to follow were many factories, suffering both from incompetent management and resentment within the labor force. Furthermore, in 1837 the Pasha implemented a major reversal of policy whereby he allowed members of his elite to own agricultural land. Those who had grown rich in the wars were given large tracts of land whose taxes had not been paid, in exchange for payment of their tax arrears and guaranteeing future tax liabilities.

Significantly, the medical establishment was not affected by these constraints. Probably alarmed by the scale of the cholera and plague epidemics and by Clot Bey's enforcement of a strict quarantine system that spared soldiers in the army, as well as workers in the Alexandria arsenal, Mehmed Ali invested even more money and effort in his medical establishments. An International Quarantine Board was established in Alexandria which was composed of members of the European consular corps; it advised the Pasha on how to combat these deadly epidemics. A large number of state-of-the-art medical books were translated from European languages (mostly French) into Arabic and were printed in the government press that had been founded in 1820. Most interestingly, a school for midwives was opened in 1832 whose graduates were expected to curb the large number of stillbirths and to help with vaccinating children against smallpox. These measures all helped to reduce the annual infant mortality rates and generally to make a significant improvement in public health and hygiene.

THE SECOND SYRIAN CRISIS

Having conducted this internal reorganization and succeeded for the time being in suppressing the different uprisings against his rule in different parts of his far-flung dominions, Mehmed Ali once again stated his intention to declare himself independent on 25 May 1838. As was the case with his first attempt four years earlier, this desire for independence was not based on any nationalist or proto-nationalist considerations, and he never claimed to be speaking on behalf of his Arabic-speaking subjects in Egypt. For example, he never argued that his subjects were resentful of Ottoman rule or that they were struggling to get rid of the Ottoman yoke as the Greeks had done in the previous decade. Rather, in his meetings with European consuls he cited two considerations: one being the fate of his many reforms, and the other the future of his family. Relaying the Pasha's anxieties, the British consul explained that Mehmed Ali could never

> ... consent that all that which he has been toiling for, and all the useful and costly establishments founded by him at an enormous expense ... revert to the Porte and to be lost at his death, and that he should have the pang of feeling that all his labours should merely have been for the Porte which would allow them to go to ruin, whilst his own children and family would be exposed to want and perhaps even to be put to death. (Kutluoğlu, 1998, 126)

In spite of these impassioned pleas, the Europeans once more opposed his quest for independence; in fact, he gradually realized that Europe – and Britain in particular – had become even less tolerant toward him in the four years that had passed since his earlier attempt at independence. It was clear that Europe's now hardened opposition had been shaped by his military exploits which had brought the Ottoman Empire to the brink of downfall, a prospect the Europeans wanted to steer well clear of in order to avoid a Europe-wide war to fight over the spoils.

SEEKING HEREDITARY RULE

Secure behind strong defensive lines, Mehmed Ali gave the European consuls his pledge that he would no longer escalate matters further militarily. Diplomatically, he changed tactics and started voicing his desire not for independence but for the hereditary succession of his authority to pass to his descendants. Over the following three years this idea of hereditary rule assumed increasing importance in Mehmed Ali's mind and he seemed, at long last, to have found a formula that would resolve his life-long concern about his ambiguous relationship with the Ottoman Empire. If only he could snatch a clear concession to that effect from the sultan and couch it in a clearly written document, ideally a *firman*, then he would have resolved his deep-seated anxiety.

However, many obstacles stood between Mehmed Ali and the attainment of his goal. Firstly, what Mehmed Ali was aspiring to – namely, that his position of governor be passed on to his descendants – had no precedent in Ottoman history. It would therefore take considerable diplomatic skill and originality of thought to find out how best to have these desires enshrined in a binding political agreement.

Secondly, contrary to his wish that this delicate matter be conducted internally through direct negotiations between himself and his sovereign, Mehmed Ali faced another serious problem – namely, intense European interference which, at times, threatened to dissipate his energy, deprive him of his significant military possessions and even dislodge him from the coveted governorship of Egypt itself.

The most serious obstacle and challenge in his bid for hereditary rule, which he first announced in the summer of 1838, were the diplomatic and political complications ensuing from a dangerous military situation that was spiraling out of control. Having given a pledge to the Europeans not to be the first to open hostilities with the Ottomans, Mehmed Ali gave his orders to Ibrahim Pasha not to give in to Ottoman provocations. However, when the Ottoman army crossed the Euphrates in mid May 1839, Mehmed Ali ordered his son to engage the Ottoman army, and on 24 June Ibrahim inflicted yet another defeat on the Ottoman army near the small town of Nizib in southern Anatolia. Things soon escalated in an alarming manner. Before news of his army's defeat could reach him, Sultan Mahmud died suddenly on 29 June. He was immediately succeeded by his seventeen-year-old son, Abdülmecid, whose first act was to pardon Mehmed Ali and to grant him the hereditary rule of Egypt. This was conditional, however, on his returning all other lands he had acquired by force – namely, Arabia, Yemen, Crete, Adana and, most notably, Syria.

Having inflicted yet another heavy military defeat on the Ottomans and, realizing that he was now negotiating with a young, inexperienced sultan, Mehmed Ali felt confident that he could, in fact, get a better deal than what was on offer. However, two further developments complicated things considerably. The first was the appointment of his old enemy, Hüsrev Pasha, to the most senior post in the Ottoman Empire, that of grand vizier. As soon as he heard this, Mehmed Ali wrote to his son telling him that the crisis was far from being over and that he expected hard times ahead (Egyptian National Archives, 1839a). Secondly – and as a direct result of Hüsrev's elevation to this important post – the grand admiral, Ahmed Fevzi, defected with his fleet to Alexandria, fearing that Hüsrev would turn against him and use his enhanced power to order his execution. In Alexandria, Fevzi presented the fleet to Mehmed Ali and urged him to capitalize on his military victory and to use his augmented naval power to sail to Istanbul and appoint himself deputy, *vekil*, to the sultan, a post with no precedent.

Mehmed Ali, however, opted for caution, realizing that with Hüsrev in the grand vizierate he was now dealing not with an inexperienced young sultan, but with a formidable foe. For years the name "Hüsrev" had become synonymous in the Pasha's mind with "the enemy" and the figure of his adversary assumed deep psychological signification. In fact, his obsession with Hüsrev bordered on the pathological and he was not even hiding this obsession from those close to him: he once told his advisors that he dreamt that he and Hüsrev were fighting each other with knives and that he had asked those around him to come to his rescue, but that none answered his plea for help. He interpreted the dream by saying that he always knew that he could never be helped by his associates and that he felt lonesome and vulnerable ('Arif, n.d., II, 11).

Given these deep-seated reasons for mistrusting Hüsrev, Mehmed Ali launched an unrelenting diplomatic onslaught to have his enemy removed from his important post: he wrote numerous letters to the viziers in Istanbul, to provincial governors, to leading military men, to members of the *ulama*, and even to the sultan's mother, insisting upon the removal of Hüsrev and arguing that only then could further bloodshed be avoided. He also wrote to Hüsrev himself telling him that he was not asking for anything except for the Syrian provinces, and that once he was granted them, he would retire to the Hijaz. In that fascinating letter he even invited his old foe to retire with him to Hijaz so that they could both spend the remaining years of their lives in peace, devoting their time to prayers and meditation and preserving good names for themselves in the Book of History (Egyptian National Archives, 1839b). Ibrahim, seeing that his father had gone too far in his obsession with Hüsrev, felt obliged to write from the frontline telling him that there were much more serious problems than Hüsrev (Egyptian National Archives, 1839c). Eventually, Ibrahim was proven right for even after Hüsrev's removal in May 1840 (most probably as a result of pressure from Mehmed Ali), the crisis persisted for months to come.

With his son's stunning victory at Nizib, Mehmed Ali had every reason to be confident that he had an uncontestable upper hand: his army was in a superb defensive position having occupied all the important cities and the strategic mountain passes in southern Anatolia; the new sultan could be easily manipulated given his young age and inexperience; and with Hüsrev out of the way he had enough men in the highest echelons of power in Istanbul who were either in his direct pay, or could easily be persuaded to do his bidding. The problem was however that if he had calculated on European disunity, as had been the case with the first Syrian crisis following the victory at Konya, this time the major European powers swiftly got their act together and handed him a Joint Note (Joint Note of 27 July 1839) telling him that they had prevailed upon the Porte to suspend all direct negotiations with Mehmed Ali and to conduct such negotiations only through their mediation. It took two years for Mehmed Ali to internalize the full implications of this Joint Note – namely, that the dispute between him and Istanbul ceased to be limited to the questions of removing Hüsrev or returning the fleet – but had become a matter of European concern. Eventually, however, Mehmed Ali rose above the narrow confines of Ottoman politics and realized that his acts had truly global implications.

Key to this second transformation of himself from an Ottoman politician to a world statesman was a sober assessment of what his military victories meant politically. In a series of impressively candid and revealing letters between him and his son, the far reaching implications of their military victories gradually became apparent to him. He first wrote to Ibrahim telling him that by insisting that he withdrew from Syria and Adana the Europeans were attempting to prevent the partition of the Ottoman Empire. This partition, he realized, would not be in his favor; in fact, it would mean that the Russians would end up taking the eastern half of the Empire by landing their troops in Istanbul, and Britain would end up occupying the western half, entrenching herself in Egypt. He then asked his son to tell him frankly what their options would be if they invaded Anatolia in order to block the Russian advance and thus remove the British pretext for occupying Egypt (Egyptian National Archives, 1839d). Ibrahim's response was shockingly candid: he told his father that he could withdraw his troops from Yemen and Arabia and thus muster 100,000 men. With this large number he could then invade Anatolia. He added that he was confident that he could defeat the Russians. The problem, he thought, lay with the Syrians and the threat they posed to his rearguard: "After our victory at Nizib and after holding celebrations all over [Syria], the Syrians are still up in arms against us ... It is certain that [they are determined] to cut our line of retreat in case we are defeated [by the Russians]" (Egyptian National Archives, 1839e).

In response, Mehmed Ali informed his son that in his most recent meeting with the British and French consuls he reiterated his insistence on holding on to Syria and Adana but left the matter of withdrawing from Crete vague (Egyptian National Archives, 1839f). Ibrahim then agreed with his father that they should hold on to Adana as tightly as they could. But he also proposed that, if need be, they could give up Arabia and return the two Holy Cities to the Sultan in exchange for keeping Adana. However, he ended by saying that if the worst were to come to the worst and if the Europeans insisted on withdrawing from Adana, then he thought that it was not worth keeping it – if keeping it meant going to war with five nations (Egyptian National Archives, 1839g).

With these very sobering calculations Mehmed Ali knew that he could not hold on to all the lands he had acquired by force. The question was, how much should he return to the sultan? And what could he get in return? For two years emissaries shuffled between Alexandria and Istanbul; Ibrahim was relaying constant information back to Egypt; and his father was regularly meeting with the European consuls. He tried his best not to be the first to blink and pushed hard to see how much land he could retain. Eventually, the stiff European opposition to his territorial expansion became abundantly clear and he realized that the one nation that had stood by him, France, did so not out of any "love for Egypt but," as he confided to his son, "because she wanted to break the political isolation that she found herself in ... My instincts about the French," he added, "have therefore been right all along. I have no choice but to comply" (Egyptian National Archives, 1840). When Palmerston invited Austria, Prussia and Russia to London, in what came to be known as the "Convention for the Pacification of the Levant" in July 1840, and when the convention issued very stern warnings to Mehmed Ali, threatening him with dire consequences if he did not return the fleet to Istanbul and order his son to withdraw from all lands he had occupied in Syria and Anatolia, Mehmed Ali still maintained a poker face and refused to budge. Seeing that the Porte had strengthened its hand by appealing to the four European nations of the London Convention, Mehmed Ali attempted to strengthen his card by accepting French mediation. Even after this mediation failed he still believed in his *fortuna* – and that things would end up as he wished.

The climax of this war of nerves was finally reached in September 1840 when the British bombarded Beirut and then landed troops there. Soon, Ibrahim's worst fears of the previous year came true: a massive uprising against Mehmed Ali's rule broke out all over Syria. Seeing that he stood to lose everything if he continued to fight, but also realizing that Palmerston had objected to the sultan's latest move of deposing him from the governorship of Egypt, and that, further, the British were willing to intercede to reinstate him in his most prized province, Mehmed Ali instructed Boghos, his loyal Armenian advisor on foreign affairs, to accept the invitation of Sir Charles Napier, the British admiral who had just arrived from Beirut, to enter into negotiations. During these negotiations Napier proposed that if the Pasha agreed to settle his differences with the sultan, returned the fleet and ordered an immediate evacuation of Syria, "such acts would ensure him the hereditary government of Egypt under the guarantee of the Allied Powers" (Kutluoğlu, 1998, 174). Judging this to be the golden opportunity he had been waiting for, Mehmed Ali immediately sent a message to his son to evacuate Syria.

JUBILATION

Ibrahim soon withdrew his massive army to Egypt and Mehmed Ali allowed the Ottoman fleet to sail to Istanbul. Shortly thereafter the Europeans interceded with the Porte to offer Mehmed Ali the longed-for promise of hereditary rule. On 20 February 1841 an emissary from the sultan arrived in Alexandria carrying the *firman* of investiture. This *firman* granted Mehmed Ali the hereditary possession of the governorship of Egypt; it set the size of the Egyptian army at 18,000; it obliged Mehmed Ali to execute all laws and treaties that the Porte had passed or entered into; and it stipulated the size of the annual tribute that Cairo had to send to Istanbul. On receiving this *firman*, Mehmed Ali was ecstatic. However, there were some important conditions that he could not accept. Significantly, he raised no objections to reducing the size of his fighting forces; his only request in this regard was to be allowed to appoint senior officers and not to leave this in the hands of the sultan as the *firman* had originally stipulated. After some negotiations his request was answered. He also managed to reduce the amount of the annual tribute. Most significantly, he strongly objected to the conditions that had allowed the sultan to retain the right to choose his successor from among his descendants in any of the direct lines. Mehmed Ali wrote back to Istanbul saying that he could not approve of this condition since it would open the door for civil war after his death (Egyptian National

Archives, 1841a). After some deliberations in Istanbul, all Mehmed
Ali's requests were positively answered and a new *firman* was issued
to that effect on 24 May which Mehmed Ali received on 7 June 1841.
Three weeks later Mehmed Ali wrote to the Sublime Porte saying,

> When I received the auspicious [*firman*] I was thankful for this
> generous bounty with which I was engulfed. I wasted no time in
> accepting it and honoring it with the appropriate grand ceremonies ...
> Once my eyes fell on it, I approached it with thankful steps and my
> lips were honored by kissing it. I was then honored by the medal
> which [the emissary] had carried with his noble hands and my chest,
> which is already full of loyalty, was thus decorated with it. All *ulama*
> and statesmen were present and the text of the *firman* was read aloud
> to them. Everyone then sang the sultan's praises and prayed for his
> long life. In order for all our subjects to enjoy this blessing, the guns
> were fired in Cairo and other cities to express our joy and happiness
> for this event. (Egyptian National Archives, 1841b)

7

TRIUMPH

At the age of seventy-one, Mehmed Ali could finally breathe a sigh of relief. The *firman* of 1841 gave him what he had been striving for ever since he landed in Egypt in 1801: an unambiguous pledge by the Ottoman sultan, backed by all major European powers, that he would continue to rule his prized province until his death, and that thereafter his descendants would inherit the governorship of Egypt and its enhanced wealth. Although this *firman* legally bestowed the governorship of Egypt on him for life, he had *de facto* been running this province independently of Istanbul since the early years of his arrival there. As might be expected, he could not handle his increasingly complex affairs single-handedly and, begrudgingly, he had to delegate some of his authority to a new bureaucracy. Even although he continued to monitor this bureaucracy closely, in the course of time it became more and more efficient and a high degree of professionalism and self-worth can be detected from the voluminous records that it generated. Key to the growth of this bureaucracy and the development of a professional civil service was the passing of a pensions statute in August 1844. This statute awarded pensions based not on the degree of proximity to the Pasha and his family but on length of service, and it therefore was an important step in the transition from household government to a modern bureaucracy.

THE PASHA AND HIS ELITE: *QUIS CUSTODIET IPSOS CUSTODES?*

Not all the Pasha's men however could be turned into civil servants, and the pensions statute alone could not transform the *zevat*, or elite, into bureaucrats. After much experimentation, Mehmed Ali started relying on law as a tool to rein in his elite members, and by the 1840s this process of legal reform had evolved into a complex and flexible legal system.

As explained above, the elite on whom Mehmed Ali relied to help him run his increasingly complex affairs was composed of members of his immediate family, friends and acquaintances from Kavala, and former slaves. It also included Coptic scribes, Armenian advisors, European technical experts and a motley assortment of Turkish-speakers who flocked to Egypt to benefit from the fabled riches of the Pasha. Holding together the disparate elements of this elite and preventing them from abusing their powers was no easy task. On the occasional report of lax behavior or improper conduct the Pasha would sprint into action, summon the wrongdoer for a hearing, and then summarily mete out a punishment that ranged from dismissal from service to death. Every now and then he would conduct an inspection tour, appearing suddenly with no prior warning, and would inflict harsh punishments on those who were unfortunate enough not to be on their guard. In a famous episode in July 1844 he sent for all his senior officials to inquire about some serious deficit in his budget that had not been reported to him. When finally some officials summoned up the courage to lay the truth before him, he exploded in a frightful frenzy and accused his son, Ibrahim, and his nephew, Şerif Pasha, of treason and greed, respectively, and announced hysterically that he had given up all hopes of reforming his men and that he would retire forthwith to Mecca (Rivlin, 1961, 70–72).

Besides the imperial *firman* of 1841 granting Mehmed Ali the governorship of Egypt, in September 1842 the young sultan Abdülmecid bestowed on him the rank of grand vizier. Savoring this new sense of legitimacy in his relationship with Istanbul, Mehmed Ali found himself dismayed by what he considered the irresponsible behavior of some members of his appointed elite. He would repeatedly plead with them to remember the *dolce vita* that they were enjoying in Egypt. And he would implore them to realize that Egypt was unlike any other country: due to its geographical location its rich soil could be harvested three, sometimes four, times a year; its strategic location, connecting India and China to the east with Europe in the north, gave it a unique position in the world. He would remind them of its long history and, having experienced two glorious moments – the time of the Pharaohs and that of the Ptolemies – he would insist that the time had come to restore this ancient land to its former glories. But this would never happen, he would conclude, if they could not give up their laziness and complacency (Egyptian National Archives, 1843).

The problem was, however, that this "laziness" and "complacency" that the Pasha often accused his retainers of were the direct product of his own style of leadership. Believing that the best government is that which combined justice and humanity with absolute power, Mehmed Ali refused to delegate any real power to his officials and they, as a result, failed to develop any sense of responsibility or feeling of public service. Even those officials who occupied senior ranks in the administration were intimidated into silence by their *veli nimet*, their Benefactor. They would sheepishly present him with their advice or opinion, but they could never take the initiative or authorize policy. They could also never be trusted with "state" matters for these were, in essence, family matters. When, for example, Mehmed Ali wrote to Ibrahim Pasha at the height of the second Syrian crisis, suggesting that he consult with his senior commanders on what they thought was the best way to negotiate with the sultan, his son responded with what the Pasha must have already known: "The generals I have with me here ... are not informed of these matters of external affairs, and if I breach these subjects with them, they will not be able to present any opinions as they have no experience with them" (Egyptian National Archives, 1839g).

Having hit upon the idea of establishing a loyal household as the best strategy with which to ensconce himself in Egypt, the problem that now confronted the Pasha was how to control the members of this household and to keep them in check. Fatherly words of advice sometimes worked; at other times, firm punishments had to be meted out. But Mehmed Ali knew that these were only palliative measures and his political instincts told him that a more lasting solution had to be found.

Mehmed Ali's familiarity with law and history here proved to be invaluable for there is compelling evidence that demonstrates his interest in learning from historical precedents. He was aware how previous dynasts, especially the Ottomans, attempted to use law in order to reinforce their rule which they accomplished through the control of members of the elite, and by trading justice to the commoners in exchange for their production of the necessary surplus. Even although Mehmed Ali was illiterate till the age of forty, he was impressively "well-read", especially in history. His advisors and translators would regularly read books to him in his spare time, and it is abundantly clear from his numerous letters – especially those to his son, Ibrahim – that his knowledge of the past considerably shaped his understanding of the present. That he was intimately familiar with Egyptian history is unquestionable and, as the source cited above shows, he was particularly intrigued by the Pharaonic and the Ptolemaic periods, and less so by the Mamluk or Ottoman ones. From the list of books printed by the Bulaq Press, which he founded in 1820, one gets a glimpse of which historical figures inspired him. Among them were Alexander the Great, Catherine the Great, Frederick the Second, and, of course, Napoleon, all of whom attracted his attention and he read their biographies to discover how they, too, had been confronted with similar questions. The story of him turning down the suggestion of translating and publishing Machiavelli's *The Prince*, because he believed that the text had nothing to teach him, is well known; less known though is the fact that he added that Ibn Khaldun was more instructive for him than the Italian political philosopher (Nallino, 2005, 130).

Above all, Mehmed Ali was thoroughly familiar with Ottoman history and justice, and how the Ottomans – that is, in the narrow sense of the word, "the house of Osman" – attempted to rein in their elite members, the *'askari* class, so as to prevent them from encroaching on the rights of their subjects, the *re'aya* (Ar. *ra'iyya*). Here the Ottoman sultans relied on the classical Islamic concept of *siyasa shar'iyya* that allowed the ruler to pass legislation that was seen as complementary to Islamic law, the *shari'a*. The Ottomans called the resulting legal codes "*qanuns*", and the increasingly sophisticated legal system that ensued from such acts of legislation were known as "*siyaset*" (Ar. *siyasa*). They thereby supplemented *shari'a* which is most vocal in private law matters with *siyaset* which is strongest in matters pertaining to public law.

Mehmed Ali was intimately familiar with these imaginative Ottoman legal experimentations. Of particular value to him were the *qanunnameh*s, or legal codes, that the sultans were repeatedly passing to prevent their elite members from abusing their privileges and encroaching on the rights of the commoners. By the 1840s the Pasha had passed many such legal codes to organize various aspects of his relationship with both his elite and his subjects. Called *qanuns*, they had no precedent within Ottoman Egypt as there had never been an Ottoman governor who had given himself such legislative rights. These codes attempted to control the elite by criminalizing some of their acts (bribery, laziness, negligence, feigning ignorance of orders and regulations, etc.) and stipulating corresponding punishments (mostly fines and imprisonment; physical punishment being reserved for the commoners). At the same time, these legal codes defined the crimes committed by the commoners and set fixed penalties for their perpetrators. Moreover, and in parallel with the traditional *shari'a* courts, special legal bodies were established and were staffed by provincial and/or bureaucratic administrators to implement these *qanuns* that the Pasha had passed. In short, by the 1840s a complex legal machinery had been created, one which was instrumental in spreading security throughout the realm, and which was characterized as much by a sophisticated engagement with classical *shari'a* principles as by an innovative way of coupling these principles with Ottoman notions of *siyaset*. Like other innovations introduced by the Pasha for his own purposes, this legal machinery eventually mushroomed in the following decades into a multi-tiered legal system and proved to be one of the most significant innovations of the Pasha.

MEHMED ALI AND THE EGYPTIANS

If the Pasha's relationship with members of his Turkish-speaking elite was a complex one – informed as it was by his incessant desire to consolidate his tenuous position in Egypt – his relationship with his subjects, that is, the Arabic-speaking residents of Egypt, was equally complex. First and foremost, he was deeply aware that ultimately it was the Egyptians – the people of the land – who were the source of his wealth. For him the Egyptian peasant, the *fellah*, was his *veli nimet*, *his* benefaction, as he once wrote to one of his officials (Sami, 1928, II, 474), playing on his own title.

There was however a deep ambiguity that shaped how Mehmed Ali viewed the Egyptians. On the one hand, he knew that whatever wealth and power he had achieved were thanks to his position as governor of Egypt. For him Egypt was his milch cow and, as indicated above, he recognized the unique qualities of this prized province, of its strategic geographic location and of its long history. Moreover, accounts of the numerous contacts the Pasha had with European visitors and, more significantly, the countless letters that he dictated to his subordinates as well as those in which he confided to his son, Ibrahim Pasha, reveal that the Pasha appeared to nurture a genuine concern for his subjects. In so far as one is able to discern it from these letters, his self-image was that of someone who had the conviction that it was his destiny to lift Egypt from the misery and darkness in which he found it on his arrival in 1801, and to lead it into the light of civilization.

On the other hand, the policies that Mehmed Ali pursued to

"civilize" and improve the lot of the Egyptians did nothing of the sort; rather, they were a source of unprecedented pauperization, suffering and misery. His monopolies policy, and the draconian measures that were taken to implement it, pushed countless peasant families into poverty as they were forced to sell the fruits of their labor cheaply to government warehouses only to buy them back at higher prices. While peasants were used to performing corvée labor on the lands of their former tax-farmers (*multazims*), Mehmed Ali's infrastructure projects required them to perform their corvée services for much longer periods each year and in areas that were often far away from their villages. Moreover, the drastic reorganization of the agricultural sector that the Pasha undertook in the 1810s caused many peasants to lose their land as they became incapable of meeting the heavier lax liabilities.

Mehmed Ali's factories were also a source of untold misery for those who worked in them. These factories have been hailed by many subsequent observers as having the potential to transform Egypt into an industrial country, enabling it to follow the models of Britain and, later, France in their industrialization efforts. They also add that, fearful of the competition the Pasha's budding industrialization experiment might have caused to its own industry, Britain opposed this experiment and successfully forced the Ottoman Empire to sign a commercial treaty – the Balta Limanı Treaty of 1838. This treaty reduced the tariff on imports to 5 percent, and removed the tariff protection that the Pasha's new factories needed, thus contributing to the collapse of what had been a promising experiment. Nevertheless, there were other serious internal problems, ranging from a lack of wood/coal supplies to power the factories' machinery and a lack of managerial and technical skills required to run them, to over-centralization of command that stifled innovation and flexibility. However, most historical accounts point to a *combination* of contributing factors, such as: the large labor force had been coerced to work against their will; the Pasha's agents did not spare women and children; the workers often supplied the motive power themselves; a strict disciplinary regime was enforced in the factories; and strikes and work stoppages were common. In short, while there is some debate as to what caused the Pasha's industrialization experiment to collapse, all sources indicate that these factories were deeply resented by the 30,000 to 40,000 workers who were dragged in to work in them.

Paradoxically, Mehmed Ali's educational policy was equally unpopular. The Pasha is often depicted as opening many schools throughout the country. The peasant children who joined these schools were not only provided with books, lodging, food and clothing all free of charge; they were also given a monthly stipend. However, a closer look reveals serious problems with the Pasha's educational policy. For one thing, the whole policy suffered from a structural imbalance caused by the fact that the advanced polytechnics (e.g. medicine, engineering, agriculture, metallurgy, etc.) were founded before the preparatory or primary schools that would supply them with the required students were opened. Given that Mehmed Ali was opposed to the idea of spreading education to the masses and was only interested in educating a limited number of children to eventually replace the foreign experts whom he had brought in at great expense (Egyptian National Archives, 1836), the number of students in his primary schools was kept very low and could not supply the advanced polytechnics with their necessary intake of students. Very often, therefore, the advanced polytechnics would take students from primary and preparatory schools before completing their course of study. The education method, moreover, put much emphasis on rote memorization and was sure to kill any creative talents that the students might have had. In addition, the schools were all run with a military discipline that manifested itself in many ways. The manner in which the children were snatched from their homes, for example, reminded people of the way young men were pressed into the army. Once "conscripted", students had to be interned in the schools and were not allowed to live with their families. Severe physical punishment (mostly flogging by whip) was regularly meted out by the teachers. Those who escaped, as well as their fathers, were subjected to harsh physical beating. Finally, upon graduation, students were not free to choose a profession of their liking but were forced to work in the Pasha's establishments. It was this bizarre way of running the schools and of supplying them with students that caused parents to resist the Pasha's educational policy: in some instances mothers even blinded their own children or cut off their fingers to prevent them from being recruited by the Pasha's agents. When Mehmed Ali was informed of these practices he ordered that some of these women be punished by drowning them in the Nile (Egyptian National Archives, 1835).

But more so than anything else, it was the Pasha's conscription policy that caused unprecedented misery to at least two generations of young Egyptian men. The tens of thousands of peasants who were dragged in to serve in Mehmed Ali's army and navy faced unspeakable horrors as they were snatched from their homes, subjected to a draconian disciplinary regime and sent to fight for years on end in wars that made no sense to them. As already mentioned above, they went to all possible ends to resist this policy that amounted to nothing less than a heavy tax in blood. After mass uprisings were ruthlessly defeated by Mehmed Ali they resorted to desperate means which often included absconding from their villages in order to avoid the press gangs, to maiming themselves, and to deserting the army altogether in spite of the harsh punishments laid down for those who were caught.

By contrast, Mehmed Ali's medical policy proved to be beneficial for the Egyptians and was to meet with the least resistance. As we have seen above, the new medical establishments that were introduced in the 1820s were directly linked to the needs of the Pasha's army. Through time however – and as with other policies – the medical policy gradually acquired a momentum of its own beyond the confines of the army and navy and its effect spilled over into civilian life; in the process, it became more acceptable to the population. People's reactions to the Pasha's medical innovations were affected by a general perception of how close these innovations were connected to the military – which they viscerally detested. For example, due to its pronounced military nature, the Qasr al-'Aini teaching hospital was the most resisted of the new medical establishments. Similarly, the quarantine system that was put in place to deal with the devastating cholera and plague epidemics was fiercely opposed as it was implemented with strict military discipline. Nevertheless, in striking contrast to hardened peasant attitudes against anything military, the various small clinics which were opened, free of charge, in urban and rural communities were patronized by the public who could receive free medical treatment especially in emergencies. Likewise, an ambitious nation-wide program to vaccinate children against smallpox was largely successful. Initially, the notion of vaccination faced resistance when peasants assumed that it was part of a sinister program to tattoo their children for future military conscription. But eventually, and especially after the army had been demobilized following the 1841 settlement, peasants' fears were dispelled; tens of thousands of young children were successfully vaccinated with the assistance of village and neighborhood shaykhs – something that helped reduce the annual infant mortality rate significantly. Finally, and once again relying on village shaykhs rather than the police or the army, the authorities were able to conduct an impressively detailed census which, taking place over a three-year period, was of personal interest to Mehmed Ali – "so that we can know the exact size of the population of our country and so that it can be a basis for its enhanced civilization" (Sami, 1928, II, 535–536).

THE PASHA'S LAST YEARS

With satisfactory outcomes to both of his long-standing concerns – those of making peace with the sultan, and of establishing control over both his elite and his subjects – Mehmed Ali spent the remaining seven years of his life ensuring that his descendants would have an ever more prosperous country over which to rule.

In 1844 he dispatched a large educational mission to France. Given that the mission was to have a military status, Süleyman Pasha, the chief-of-staff of the army, was ordered to select seventy suitable young men to be sent to France. In Paris a special school was chosen to house the student group, which included two future rulers of Egypt: Said Pasha, Mehmed Ali's own son (b. 1822; r. 1854–1863), and Ismail Pasha, Ibrahim Pasha's son (b. 1830; r. 1863–1879).

The following year, as already mentioned, the Pasha ordered the undertaking of a general census of the country – a modern one in that, rather than simply households, it counted individuals. Amounting to something over 5300 registers, this census is preserved in the Egyptian National Archives and includes data on household composition, sex, age, religion, occupation, ethnic origin, marriage and polygamy, migration, and physical infirmities. The census took three years to compile and is an eloquent testimony of the degree of precision and self-confidence that the Pasha's administration had achieved, as well as its ability to penetrate deeply into Egyptian society.

In 1847 Mehmed Ali laid the foundation stone of a huge infrastructure project that would be associated with his name for generations to come. Constructed at the apex of the Delta in order to regulate the flow of the Nile in Lower Egypt, this project was known as the Nile Barrages or *al-Qanatir al-Khayriyya*. The project had its origins in a plan submitted more than ten years earlier and for which the Pasha had contemplated using the stones of the great pyramid in Giza. His chief French engineer, however, succeeded in dissuading him from the extraordinary idea. After losing heart with the project for some years, Mehmed Ali resumed interest and was still hopeful that this huge project might be completed during his lifetime.

The Pasha's last years were witness to an improvement in relations with the British. In 1843 the British government decided to send a steamship as a token of gratitude; and Queen Victoria bestowed a rare honor by sending her personal portrait. He sent his son, Ibrahim Pasha, on a trip to London and Paris, and even contemplated a similar trip himself, having been reassured by Lord Palmerston that he would be graciously received by the Queen. However, ill health prevented him from undertaking such a trip. His cordial relations with France became even warmer and he struck up a personal friendship with

King Louis-Philippe. In 1845 the king sent him a tower clock that was installed in the courtyard of the huge Istanbul-style mosque that the Pasha was having constructed for himself atop the Citadel. This clock was in exchange for one of the two obelisks, originally from Alexandria, which the Pasha had earlier presented to France as a gift.

In the summer of 1846 Mehmed Ali paid his first and only trip to the Ottoman capital. He was then seventy-six years old – three times the age of Sultan Abdülmecid and infinitely more experienced and renowned than the young sultan. During the month-long visit from 19 July to 17 August, Mehmed Ali received a very warm welcome and past grudges seem to have been forgotten between the sultan and his vassal. He even paid a courtesy visit to his old rival, Hüsrev Pasha, who had lost all his power and much of his wealth. On his way back to Egypt he stopped at his birthplace, Kavala, and visited the charitable school he had founded there.

Soon after his return to Egypt Mehmed Ali's health finally gave out and he became no longer capable of making sense, let alone running a country. In 1847 the daily affairs of the government were taken over by Ibrahim, now in his late fifties and not in good health himself. Early in 1848 both father and son went on convalescing trips to the Mediterranean. Mehmed Ali's steamer was supposed to take him to Malta and then Marseilles, but news of the French revolution of that year forced him to head for Naples where he met his son for the last time. On hearing that Louis-Philippe had been deposed, Mehmed Ali, now in the grip of advanced senility, contemplated a military expedition to France to reinstate his friend on the throne. In the meantime, Ibrahim had journeyed on to Istanbul to have the governorship of Egypt conferred on himself on the grounds that his father had become too infirm to rule. Barely a few weeks later, Ibrahim died on 12 September 1848. News of his death was kept from the ailing Pasha while urgent dispatches were hastily sent to Abbas Pasha, Mehmed Ali's grandson, who was in Arabia and who was second in line, asking him to return to Egypt without delay. On 10 November 1848 Abbas was instated by Istanbul as governor of Egypt.

Mehmed Ali fell into ever deeper senility during his last months, and his general health was not helped by the doses of silver nitrate that his doctors were administering to him for dysentery. Even in the rare moments of consciousness when he barely made sense, his mind would still spin off on some fantastic scheme, the most bizarre of which being a planned invasion of China. On 2 August 1849 his weak body finally surrendered and he died in his palace in Alexandria close to mid-day. From there the coffin was transported by river up the Nile to Cairo; the funeral cortège departed from Qasr al-Nil Palace overlooking the Nile across the city to the Sayyida Zaynab Mosque where prayers were read. The body was then led up to the Citadel and was buried in the mosque carrying the Pasha's name. The funeral was led by Said Pasha, Mehmed Ali's son; all the surviving members of the family except the new governor, Abbas Pasha, joined the funeral cortège. The shops, however, were not closed, the public seeming to prefer to get on with their lives as if nothing had happened. Very few Egyptians in fact joined the procession for the funeral of the man who had ruled them for nearly half a century.

After Abbas's death in 1854, the governorship of Egypt passed to his uncle, Said Pasha, who was Mehmed Ali's son and who was next in line given that he was the eldest male survivor of Mehmed Ali. Upon his death in 1863 he was followed by Ismail Pasha, Ibrahim Pasha's son, who managed to extract a new *firman* from Istanbul changing the rules of succession to remain within his own line. Henceforth Ibrahim's line ruled Egypt for another ninety years until the whole Mehmed Ali dynasty was deposed in 1952 by a military coup led by Colonel Gamal Abdel-Nasser.

8

THE PASHA'S MULTIPLE
LEGACIES

To say that much happened during Mehmed Ali's forty-three-year reign is hardly an exaggeration. Within the Ottoman Empire itself, Mehmed Ali's tenure spanned the reigns of four successive sultans. An even greater number of grand viziers acquired, and then lost, their posts whilst Mehmed Ali was busy consolidating his power in Egypt. In a similar fashion his arch rival, Hüsrev Pasha, rose to great heights in the empire in Egypt but, unlike him, he lost it all and ended up in prison in July 1840 charged with corruption and embezzlement. By the 1840s Mehmed Ali was the single most senior, most powerful and longest serving official throughout the whole of the Ottoman Empire.

The pace and nature of change that had taken place in Egypt under the Pasha's long reign was even more momentous. Most significantly, the old ruling Mamluk aristocracy had literally been wiped out and in their place Mehmed Ali, as we have shown, skillfully created a political elite that was formed around his own family and his extended household. This had enormous political and social significance. Until then power in Egypt had traditionally revolved around leading Mamluk households while the governor, who was sent from Istanbul, had little say in how the province was run. These leading households acted not only as centers of economic and political power but also extended their patronage to poets, architects and scientists. However, the internecine warfare that characterized much of the politics of Mamluk households dissipated their energies and prevented any real accumulation of power, wealth or culture. ·

By replacing the multiple Mamluk households with a single one, Mehmed Ali brought change to the political map of Egypt forever because all the potential wealth of the country could now be harnessed to serve a single political agenda, an agenda that was increasingly being shaped on the domestic front rather than from Istanbul. Unlike previous governors whose tenure in Egypt rarely exceeded a few years, Mehmed Ali had the luxury of time to invest the long-term accumulated wealth garnered from Egypt's land and its people in projects which had as their main purpose the consolidation of the Pasha's household and the enhancement of his wealth. The result was a centralization of power not witnessed in Egypt for centuries. In short, a strong centralized state had been born.

Given the long years of the Pasha's reign and the many dramatic events it witnessed, it is natural that opinion is divided on how to judge his legacy. Even during his lifetime, Mehmed Ali's policies proved to be just as controversial domestically as they were in Istanbul and in Europe. In Istanbul, Kavalalı Mehmed Ali Paşa – as the Pasha was referred to in Ottoman sources – was a source of fear, derision, envy and fascination. Personifying the single most dangerous threat to the Ottoman Empire in its long history, Mehmed Ali was feared by the viziers in Istanbul who were dismayed at how this unknown pasha had succeeded in raising an army that had managed to penetrate deep into the central heartlands of Anatolia, threatening the very seat of the sultanate itself. While Ottoman archival sources are replete with correspondence from Sultan Mahmud and his viziers that express their loathing and disgust of this upstart who dared to defy the sultan's orders in this most flagrant manner, they also reveal a certain degree of fascination at Mehmed Ali's ability to beat them at their own program of reform and centralization. In this way the famous *Tanzimat* reform program – launched in Istanbul in 1839 and introducing important legal, financial and military reforms to the Ottoman Empire – can be seen as having been inspired by earlier innovations that Mehmed Ali had successfully introduced in Egypt, and not simply as a reflection of western pressure and influence on Ottoman politicians.

Similarly, Mehmed Ali was also a source of both fascination and disgust in Europe. At the risk of oversimplification it could be said that many French commentators were intrigued by a man whom they saw as an oriental version of Napoleon – one who was himself inspired by the French emperor and who employed numerous Frenchmen, many of whom had previously served in Napoleon's army. The British, on the other hand, saw Mehmed Ali's policies as a serious challenge to the British Empire and considered his military expansionism to threaten the very existence of the Ottoman Empire which, in turn, was considered a bulwark against a possible Russian advance on India – the most prized of British overseas possessions. Naturally there were divisions within each of these European camps. For example, while the Frenchman Clot Bey, Mehmed Ali's chief medical advisor, published a highly laudatory account of the Pasha's rule (Clot Bey, 1840), his fellow countryman, Pierre Hamont, who was director of the Veterinary School, was very harsh in his own judgment which he published in 1843 (Hamont, 1843). In a similar fashion, the contemporary British opinion on the Pasha was also divided. The British foreign secretary, Lord Palmerston, for example, despised Mehmed Ali and once wrote to his ambassador in Paris saying, "For my part I hate Mehemet Ali, whom I consider as nothing but an ignorant barbarian … I look upon his boasted civilization as the arrantest humbug; and I believe that he is as great a tyrant and oppressor as ever made a people wretched" (Temperley, 1964, 89). By contrast, many British travelers who had a chance to visit Egypt and to meet with the Pasha were mesmerized by him and have left behind positive accounts (Measor, 1844; Wilde, 1844; Waghorn, 1843; Wilkinson, 1843). Most notably, John Bowring, the British MP who was sent by Palmerston himself on an official mission to report on Mehmed Ali's administration, and the sources of his fabled wealth that allowed him to raise such large armies, ended up drafting a highly detailed report that was not devoid of praise for the Pasha. Anxious that the report might make an undesired positive impact on MPs and his colleagues in the cabinet, Lord Palmerston deleted considerable portions of it (Bowring, 1840; Bartle, 1964).

In Egypt the debate over Mehmed Ali's legacy has continued unabated since the Pasha's own time. For example, 'Abd al-Rahman al-Jabarti, the famous historian who witnessed the first fifteen years of Mehmed Ali's reign, spared no effort in depicting the hardship felt by both his own class of tax-farmers (*multazims*) as well as by the urban and rural poor as a result of the Pasha's policies. It was only natural, therefore, for the Pasha to refuse to publish Jabarti's *'Aja'ib* in his newly established press, with the result that this monumental historical work was not published until 1880.

The Pasha's direct descendants, who continued to govern Egypt for a century after his death, were naturally very keen on defending the founder of their dynasty from any criticism and they regularly depicted him as the originator of all that was good and beneficial in Egypt. Among other things, they tended to endow him with extraordinary qualities, effectively creating a pedestal upon which his memory was raised. Even although the Pasha insisted during his lifetime that "Mahomed [*sic*] Ali is no Pasha – has no title – is plain Mahomed Ali", and added that "I have never put on my seal any other inscription than Mahomed Ali" (British National Archives, 1826), his son, Said Pasha (r. 1854–1863), felt it necessary to issue a decree that his father be referred to in government correspondence by no other name or title than the Persian one of *"jennatmakaan"*, which means "Dwelling in Paradise" (Egyptian National Archives, 1860).

A further qualitative change came in how Mehmed Ali was perceived with the arrival of the Pasha's grandson, Khedive Ismail, for he always insisted that his grandfather was not only founding a dynasty, but with it also a "civilization". In a speech inaugurating his new parliament in 1866 Ismail argued that when his grandfather came to Egypt "he found it without any trace of civilization, and he found its people deprived of security and comfort," and so he devoted himself "to making the people secure and to civilizing the country"

(Cuno, 2000 and 2005). In emphasizing his grandfather's pioneering efforts, Ismail also depicted Mehmed Ali as a solitary figure concerned about nothing but the welfare of his own people, a theme that the Pasha himself had tried to convey many times in conversation with his European visitors (K. Fahmy, 1998, 38–41).

This image of a solitary figure who was ahead of his times, little understood by his own people and striving against all odds to lift Egypt from its worn-down and decrepit state, went hand-in-hand with a growing tendency to ignore the Ottoman context that governed Mehmed Ali's thought and action. With the rise of nationalist thought towards the end of the nineteenth century, the would-be independent nation-state status of Egypt was assumed to be a given entity – an entity, moreover, that had long been struggling to achieve independence from what was then increasingly seen as a prolonged period of oppressive and alien Ottoman rule. And it was Mehmed Ali – now referred to as Muhammad 'Ali, using the Arabic pronunciation of his name – who was perceived as the one who had been destined during his lifetime to deliver the impetus towards this precious independence.

A key role in the transformation of the image of Mehmed Ali from that of a founder of a dynasty to that of a proto-nationalist leader was undertaken by the Pasha's great-grandson, King Fouad (r. 1917–1936) (Di Capua, 2004). King Fouad launched an ambitious historiographical project that aimed at writing the history of his family by concentrating on the activities of his paternal ancestors – Mehmed Ali, Ibrahim and Ismail. Fouad dispatched numerous missions to European archives to hand-copy select correspondence related to his ancestors. When they arrived in Cairo these documents were translated and arranged chronologically and were thus removed from their original archival context; under the auspices of the palace they were then published in eighty-seven lavish volumes. One central theme runs through these publications – namely, the depiction of Mehmed Ali and his son Ibrahim Pasha as struggling to secure Egypt's independence through military and diplomatic efforts. King Fouad also ordered the transfer to his own palace of a select set of documents that had been housed in an old archival depository in the

Cairo Citadel. European archivists were then hired to catalogue and translate these documents, thus creating what came to be known as the Royal Archives. Once again, the main concern in selecting, cataloguing and translating these documents was to depict Mehmed Ali, Ibrahim and Ismail (much less so Abbas and Said) as striving not to reinforce dynastic rule in Egypt, but to found a modern Egyptian nation-state. One of King Fouad's most effective efforts in eulogizing his great-grandfather was to commission Henry Dodwell, a British academic historian of colonial India, to write a study of his great-grandfather. The result, *The Founder of Modern Egypt: A Study of Muhammed Ali*, was published in 1931 and proved to be a classic; its influence in casting Mehmed Ali in the title role increased even further when an Arabic translation appeared a few years later (Dodwell, 1931). As a professor in the University of London, much weight and credence was given to Dodwell's biography of Mehmed Ali. However, he failed to mention the crucial fact that he had been on the payroll of King Fouad. He also did not reveal the degree to which he depended on the staff of the royal palace to supply him with his sources, even though this dependence must have been complete, given that he knew neither Arabic nor Turkish.

The Pasha's image received a significant boost with the publication of 'Abd Al-Rahman al-Rafi'i's *'Asr Muhammad 'Ali (Mehmed Ali's reign)* (Al-Rafi'i, 1930). A professional politician and member of the Egyptian Senate, al-Rafi'i was also a prolific writer and his study on the Pasha's long reign constituted only one part in a large multi-volume survey of the "Egyptian national movement". In this study, which has been in print since its publication in 1930, al-Rafi'i's main protagonist is the "Egyptian people" whom the Pasha is depicted as listening to and whose lot he was striving to improve. Al-Rafi'i takes the national movement as his principal unit of analysis; accordingly the Ottoman Empire comes across as an alien, oppressive colonizer and Mehmed Ali is depicted as struggling to get rid of the Ottoman yoke. Al-Rafi'i observes that Mehmed Ali was suited for the proto-nationalist role in which he cast him, given what he saw as the Pasha's efforts to keep Britain's imperialist designs at bay.

When the Egyptian University was founded in 1925 Egyptian academic historians set out to compete with both the palace historians, whom they saw as overemphasizing the role of the dynasty in "modernizing" Egypt, and historians such as al-Rafiʻi whom they saw as amateurs who were not in the habit of using archival sources and satisfied themselves instead with newspapers clippings and travelers' accounts. By contrast, Shafik Ghorbal, the doyen of the academic historians, spent years in European archives studying documents pertaining to the early years of Mehmed Ali in Egypt. The result was *The Beginnings of the Egyptian Question and the Rise of Mehmet Ali* (1928), written originally as a B.A. thesis under the supervision of Arnold Toynbee. In *Beginnings* Ghorbal was keen to test out his supervisor's idea of "challenge and response" on Egyptian history, and the result is a view of Mehmed Ali as the real mover in early nineteenth-century Egypt with, curiously, little or no role played by "the Egyptian people". Upon his return to Egypt and after being appointed as the first Egyptian professor of history, Ghorbal directed his students to study various aspects of social life during the Pasha's long reign. Unlike al-Rafiʻi who had been denied access to the Royal Archives, these students produced theses and dissertations that were heavily dependent on archives housed in the royal palace. Also unlike al-Rafiʻi's romanticized notion of the "Egyptian people" as prime movers of history, these young scholars highlighted key institutions that they took as pivotal in bringing modernity to Egypt, e.g. the printing press (Radwan, 1953), schools ('Abd al-Karim, 1938; see also Heyworth-Dunne, 1938), industry (al-Jiritli, 1952; see also M. Fahmy, 1954) and agriculture (al-Hitta, 1936; see also Baer, 1962; and Barakat, 1977). However, they, too, were not granted unrestricted access to the archives, and given their lack of Ottoman Turkish, the language in which most of the documents from Mehmed Ali's time was written, they were heavily dependent on the staff of the royal archives — just as Dodwell before them had been. The result was invariably a series of studies that cast Mehmed Ali in a consistently positive light. Most crucially, the heavy price paid by Arabic-speaking Egyptians as a result of the Pasha's many innovations was

either not explored at all or was even justified as a necessary compo-
nent in the modernization process of Egypt.

Curiously, later in his career Shafik Ghorbal produced another
study of Mehmed Ali. *Muhammad 'Ali al-Kabir* (1944) was a highly
laudatory biography of the "great" Pasha, in which Ghorbal cast
Mehmed Ali in the role not of the founder of modern Egypt but of the
"regenerator" of the Ottoman Empire. This interesting twist followed a slightly earlier one by George Antonius in his classic *The Arab
Awakening* (1938). In this study Mehmed Ali and Ibrahim Pasha are
seen as motivated by a desire to unify all Arabic-speaking subjects of
the Ottoman Empire under one political leadership, a strange claim
given that both men never spoke Arabic (although it is difficult to
imagine that they did not understand any spoken Arabic).

After the 1952 coup that deposed the Mehmed Ali dynasty and
declared Egypt a republic the following year, another twist occurred
in the historical portrayal of Mehmed Ali. Even although the revolutionary regime was vociferously against the *ancien régime*, a certain
ambiguity regarding Mehmed Ali (as opposed to his successors) can be
detected: on the one hand, he was seen as the founder of the dynasty
that the coup set out to depose; on the other, the thesis of Mehmed
Ali as the founder of modern Egypt was accepted, albeit grudgingly.
For example, the National Charter of 1962, in which the Nasser
regime gave its clearest articulation of its own ideology, stated that
"there is a near consensus on seeing Muhammad 'Ali as the founder of
modern Egypt". However, the Charter also argued that Mehmed Ali's
personal adventures and his constant disregard for the people's well-
being and wishes cost Egypt dearly (Abdel-Nasser, 1962).

WHAT WENT WRONG?

In emphasizing how Mehmed Ali's "personal adventures impeded the
momentum of Egyptian awakening" by opening the doors for foreign
interference, the Charter made a comparison with modern Japan
whose modern advance has ostensibly been made possible by the

absence of foreign influence. This interesting comparison with Japan was not restricted to the Charter and it is in fact an oft-quoted parallel in academic and popular discussions of Mehmed Ali. Its main purpose is to explain the reasons why Egypt lagged behind while Japan forged ahead, even although Egypt had started its modernization under Mehmed Ali a full half-century before the Japanese Meiji reform was launched. The Charter's response to this intriguing question was to argue that Mehmed Ali had been suspicious of the "people" and ignored their well-being. In this the Charter seems to have been following a powerful argument made some sixty years earlier at the turn of the twentieth century by Muhammad 'Abduh, the renowned and influential Muslim reformer.

In an interesting article that he wrote on the centennial anniversary of Mehmed Ali's coming to power, Muhammad 'Abduh raised the question of what would have happened had Mehmed Ali not decimated the Mamluks and their local allies. In a highly conjectural yet thoughtful answer to this interesting question, 'Abduh surmised that an indigenous middle class would have evolved, a middle class that could have acted as a check to absolute power and could have led the national movement to resist British imperialism. However, 'Abduh's argument continued,

> with the army on his side, and being instinctively cunning, Mehmed Ali annihilated the Mamluk ringleaders. He then used another group to defeat his former allies. Eventually, and after defeating all political factions, he directed his energy against the leaders of the powerful households till not one head could utter the word "I". He continued this practice until the people had been entirely demoralized and were drained of every last ounce of their courage. Anyone who knew his own self-worth either had his head chopped off or was banished to meet his own death in distant lands. ('Abduh, 1902, 179)

It was Mehmed Ali's eradication of the indigenous middle classes and his monopolization of power, 'Abduh argued, that allowed Egypt to fall easily into the grips of Britain in 1882. Compared to the stiff resistance the French, under Bonaparte, had faced when they attempted to occupy Egypt eight decades earlier, the British had a relatively easy time because Mehmed Ali's regime had extinguished the proud, independent spirit that had once animated the Egyptian people and cowed their leaders into submission.

In 1961 an important study on the Pasha's internal policies, especially those related to agriculture, appeared in English. Helen Rivlin's *The Agricultural Policy of Muhammad 'Ali in Egypt* offered a highly critical account of the Pasha's rule (Rivlin, 1961). Relying on European consular reports, travelers' accounts, and contemporary Arabic and European publications, Rivlin's account offers a critical view of various aspects of Mehmed Ali's economic policies and highlights both the endemic corruption, mismanagement and inefficiency of the Pasha's administration, as well as the degree to which the peasants suffered at the hands of this administration.

Less than a decade later, Roger Owen's study, *Cotton and the Egyptian Economy* (1969) appeared, offering a wealth of statistical information that had not been available before. It also offered a sober analysis of commercial activities, agricultural practices, fluctuations in government income and, in general, the economic policies pursued by Mehmed Ali and his successors. Owen's overall hypothesis is that while the introduction of long-staple cotton led to rising incomes and growing trade, it did not lead to a diversification of production through the emergence of new sectors, nor did it bring about significant structural changes. In short, "there was growth, but not development". In attempting to answer the question of why Mehmed Ali and his successors failed to establish firm bases for self-sustaining economic growth, Owen was skeptical of the argument that put the blame on foreign capitalism, whether mercantile or industrial. In a short but illuminating conclusion he, too, compares the experiences of Egypt and Japan to draw attention to such factors as the different roles played by the government in designing policies that had economic development as their prime target, and the differences in factor endowments between both countries.

By contrast, in her 1984 study of Mehmed Ali, *Egypt in the Reign of Muhammad Ali*, A.L. al-Sayyid Marsot argues that the Pasha was not successful in his project because of staunch British resistance (Al-Sayyid Marsot, 1984). In this study the Pasha is seen as motivated, first and foremost, by a mercantilist mindset that aimed at maximizing local production and exports and minimizing imports. This mercantilist mindset, Marsot argues, necessitated launching an ambitious industrial policy, one which appeared to be based on sound principles, and to have been the main reason behind military expansion. It was this potentially successful economic policy and the prospect of establishing an industrial base on the banks of the Nile which led to British hostility. Alarmed by the possibility of having to compete with Egyptian products in the markets of the East Mediterranean, Marsot continues, Britain was determined to fight the Pasha, roll back his territorial expansion and close down his factories. This became possible when Britain signed a commercial treaty with the Ottoman Empire in 1838 banning monopolies throughout the Empire and thus undermining one of the principal means by which the Pasha attempted to protect his nascent industry. Marsot argues that the final death blow came with the 1841 *firman* which robbed Egypt of its colonies and reduced the army to a mere one-tenth of its former size. With the loss of these markets that the colonies and the army represented, the Pasha's dream of establishing an industrial base in Egypt was frustrated. "Industrialization was doomed to fail in Egypt," Marsot concludes, "not through the shortcomings of the Egyptians, but because of external European pressures which used Ottoman legal control over Egypt to kill off any potential rivalry to their own industrial ventures" (Al-Sayyid Marsot, 1984, 259).

As plausible as it may appear, Marsot's explanation that the collapse of Mehmed Ali's manufacturing experiment was due to the signing of the 1838 Treaty leaves many questions unanswered. For one thing – as was argued by Owen in an earlier study (Owen, 1981, 75) – there is evidence that the Pasha started closing his factories down in 1837, a full year before the signing of the Treaty. For another, Mehmed Ali's factories did not need high protective tariffs to survive since the Pasha had multiple administrative means at his disposal to protect his industries, and these were not given up after 1838.

Furthermore, as discussed at the end of Chapter Six above, when Mehmed Ali was informed of the terms of the 1841 *firman*, he raised no objections about what that *firman* said concerning either the necessity of implementing the terms of the 1838 Treaty or the obligation to reduce the size of his army to 18,000. Rather, what preoccupied the Pasha for the four months from February to May 1841 were the terms of succession within his family following his death. Had Mehmed Ali been concerned about his manufacturing industry and the supposed impact that the 1838 Treaty had on them, one must surmise that he would have attempted to alter the terms of the 1841 *firman* that touched on that issue just as he had successfully managed to alter the other succession terms.

Furthermore, even although Marsot used Egyptian archival sources to support her case, she did so without paying enough attention to how they had been selected and doctored in the first place. For even although she consulted these documents in the Egyptian National Archives, the manner in which they had been selected, catalogued and translated from Ottoman Turkish into Arabic had not been altered when they were moved from the royal palace. As was the case with the earlier generation of Egyptian nationalist historians who had produced their 1930s and 1940s studies on various aspects of Mehmed Ali's policy, Marsot relied heavily on an archival collection that had been carefully selected by King Fouad's archivists to portray the Pasha's reign in the most positive light possible. And finally, no doubt it was these carefully chosen archival sources that partly explain the manner in which Marsot brushes aside the question of the heavy social cost paid by peasants during the Pasha's reign (Al-Sayyid Marsot, 1984, 243–244 and 261).

Doubts about the traditional view of the Pasha which until then had bordered on the eulogistic were strengthened by the discovery during the 1980s of new archival sources that shed light on various aspects of the Pasha's reign. Being independent of the Pasha's administration, the *shari'a* court records had not been transferred from former archival depositories to the Royal Archives back in the 1930s when it was established by King Fouad. The records of these courts were starting to become available for use by historians in the 1970s and 1980s when they became a vital source of new information on various aspects of social, cultural and economic life from as early as the sixteenth century. Judith Tucker used these records in her 1985 study, *Women in Nineteenth-Century Egypt*, and the result was a detailed picture of the hardships that befell women and the family as a result of the economic policies pursued in the first half of the nineteenth century. Similarly, making use of the same sources, Kenneth Cuno has described in vivid detail the impact of the Pasha's policy on peasants and has convincingly revised the traditional thesis whereby Mehmed Ali was credited for introducing private property in land (Cuno, 1992).

Recent historians with a knowledge of both the Arabic and Turkish languages have managed to get around the problem of doctored or otherwise faulty translations left behind by King Fouad's archivists. The result has been a series of new studies that offer a new perspective on various aspects of the Pasha's reign which did not receive the attention of earlier historians. One key area was that of legal reform where the picture that is now emerging makes important connections between innovations in the fields of law and justice and developments within the larger Ottoman Empire (e.g. Peters, 2005, 133–141). These new sources have also enabled historians to highlight the heavy price paid by subaltern Egyptians as a result of the Pasha's policies (K. Fahmy, 1997, 1998; see also Kuhnke, 1990; contrast with Sonbol, 1991). Using archival material housed in the Egyptian National Archives and other depositories in Cairo, Robert Hunter's 1984 study, *Egypt Under the Khedives*, proved invaluable when it came to shedding light on the creation of the bureaucracy and the rise of a professional civil service (Hunter, 1984).

With regard to the Pasha's industrial policy, Pascale Ghazaleh's study "Masters of the Trade: Crafts and Craftspeople in Cairo, 1750–1850", was the first to pry into and prise open, so to speak, one of the Pasha's industrial establishments (Ghazaleh, 1999). Relying on a single payroll register for one factory in Cairo that dates from 1823, she presented one of the most detailed accounts so far of the working conditions in these factories. Although brief, Ghazaleh's analysis convincingly offers one important conclusion – namely, that labor in these industrial establishments was not free as forces of the market were always supplemented by severe police action that maintained the laborers in the factories by force.

The historiography of Mehmed Ali therefore has been and continues to be animated by questions that go beyond the confines of the Pasha's historical time, questions such as: how can Egypt make the transition from agricultural nation to an industrialized one? Should the state lead the way for economic development? What role should be given to religion in the process of reform and modernization? Behind these not inconsiderable contemporary questions is an even larger one: what went wrong in the past? Having seen one of the earliest and most ambitious attempts at state-run development come to a dramatic end, some historians have put the blame squarely on Britain and her imperial designs on the region. Others have highlighted internal problems that, in and of themselves, would sooner or later have brought this experiment to a standstill. These are obviously political questions that no amount of archival research will unravel. There will always be, for example, those who will consider the social cost paid by the Egyptian people during the Pasha's reign to have been too high, regardless of the benefits that may have accrued to later generations or to the country at large, at the same time as there will always be those who maintain that any price is justified in order for the "nation" to become modern.

As fascinating as all these questions may be, they ultimately address what is really a misformed question: "What went wrong with Mehmed Ali's experiment?" This is in fact a non-question for the simple reason that nothing went wrong. Only if we ignore the Ottoman context in which the Pasha thought and acted, and only if we impose on him questions deriving from another time period in which nationalism became the name of the game, can the Pasha's project appear as a failure. But as this book has attempted to show, the Pasha actually succeeded in his endeavors beyond his wildest dreams. Having arrived in Egypt at the beginning of the nineteenth century as an inexperienced young man – without money, without military glory, without illustrious ancestry, without even a knowledge of Arabic – and with no patron in Istanbul who would take him under his wing, he managed during his long tenure to overcome all these serious handicaps and to end up as sole, and legitimate, ruler of Egypt, one of the wealthiest provinces in the Ottoman Empire. From his humble origins in Kavala he rose to the challenge soon after landing in Egypt of transforming himself into the astute politician he was to become. In his sixties he once again reinvented himself, casting himself in the role of international statesman and managing, against all odds, to pass Egypt on to a dynasty whose legitimacy had been acknowledged by all the leading powers at that time. After his death this dynasty ruled Egypt for a further one hundred years. Having succeeded in his life-long project to secure himself in Egypt and to establish a position that he could hand down to his descendants, Mehmed Ali had every reason to be content with what he had accomplished during his lifetime.

The same, sadly, cannot be said for the millions of Egyptian people whose lot, as a direct result of what Mehmed Ali actually did achieve, was that of hardship and suffering. The Pasha might not have arrived in Egypt with the intention of improving their lot but with the passage of time, however, he came to see himself as destined to do exactly that. In spite of his providential self-image, there is compelling evidence to suggest that his Arabic-speaking Egyptian subjects suffered more under his tenure than they and their predecessors before them had ever suffered in centuries, if not millennia. The one single innovation introduced by Mehmed Ali that the ordinary person was able to benefit from was the free medical service which filtered down to them almost coincidentally but which did little to offset the atrocities that his other innovations entailed. His policies of high taxation, monopolies, forced labor and conscription were as unprecedented in their ferocity as they were brutal in their implementation and duration. For nearly fifty years Egyptians resisted Mehmed Ali's draconian policies with the only possible means at their disposal – their physical labor and their collective will – and these they made use of by participating in mass uprisings; absconding from their villages; deserting from his army, his schools, and his factories; attacking his officials; and most dramatically, harming their own bodies to deny him the benefit of their labor. It is hardly surprising then, that when Mehmed Ali finally died, few of his Egyptian subjects bothered to join his funeral procession.

BIBLIOGRAPHY

ARCHIVAL SOURCES

British National Archives, F.O. 78/89, Salt, 20 April 1817.

British National Archives, F.O. 78/147, Salt, 24 September 1826.

British National Archives, F.O. 78/160, Salt, 30 June 1827 a.

British National Archives, F.O. 78/160, Salt, 3 March 1827 b.

Egyptian National Archives, Dhawat, carton no. 1, doc. no. 2, 21 Dhu al-Hijja 1226/6 January 1812.

Egyptian National Archives, Bahr Barra, carton no. 3, doc. no. 6, 30 Muharram 1228/2 February 1813.

Egyptian National Archives, Ma'iyya Saniyya, reg. no. S/1/50/2 (old no. 10), doc. no. 340, 19 Dhu al-Qa'da 1237/8 August 1822.

Egyptian National Archives, Ma'iyya Turki, reg. no. 139, letter no. 97, 19 Jumada I 1251/12 September 1835.

Egyptian National Archives, 'Abdeen, reg. 212, doc. no. 277, 29 Dhu al-Hijja 1251/16 April 1836.

Egyptian National Archives, 'Abdeen, reg. S/5/47/2 (old no. 6), letter no. 149, 26 Rabi' II 1255/9 July 1839 a.

Egyptian National Archives, 'Abdeen, reg. S/5/47/2 (old no. 6), letter no. 208, 5 Jumada II 1255/16 August 1839 b.

Egyptian National Archives, Sham, carton no. 48 (old no. 'Abdeen 258), letter no. 53, 24 Jumada II 1255/4 September 1839 c.

Egyptian National Archives, 'Abdeen, reg. S/5/47/2 (old no. 6), letter no. 212, 12 Jumada II 1255 / 23 August 1839 d.

Egyptian National Archives, Sham, carton no. 48 (old no. 'Abdeen, 258), letter no. 53, 24 Jumada II 1255/4 September 1839 e.

Egyptian National Archives, 'Abdeen, reg. S/5/47/2 (old no. 6), letter no. 256, 11 Sha'ban 125/20 October 1839 f.

Egyptian National Archives, Sham, carton no. 49, (old no. 'Abdeen 258), letter no. 140, 19 Sha'ban 1255/28 October 1839 g.

Egyptian National Archives, 'Abdeen, reg. S/5/51/10 (old no. 214), letter no. 466, 2 Rajab 1256/30 August 1840.

Egyptian National Archives, 'Abdeen, reg. S/5/54/5 (old no. 8), letter no. 39, 6 Muharram 1257/28 February 1841 a.

Egyptian National Archives, 'Abdeen, reg. S/5/54/5 (old no. 8), letter no. 40, 7 Jumada I 1257/27 June 1841 b.

Egyptian National Archives, Diwan Madaris, carton no. 2, doc. no. 69, on 4 Jumada II 1259/2 July 1843.

Egyptian National Archives, Sham, carton no. 49 (old no. 'Abdeen 258), letter no. 140, 19 Sha'ban 1255/28 October 1839 g.

Egyptian National Archives, Diwan al-Jihadiyya, reg. M/14/1, Exalted Order to al-Qal'a al-Sa'idiyya, p. 2, no. 5, 4 Ramadan 1276/26 March 1860.

CONTEMPORARY SOURCES

'Arif, Mehmed (Bey). "*'Ibar al-Bashar fi al-Qarn al-Thalith 'Ashr*," MS, Egyptian National Archives, Abhath, carton no. 149 (2 vols.).

Bowring, John. "Report on Egypt and Candia." *Parliamentary Papers*, v. 21, 1840, 1–236.

Clot Bey, Antoine B. *Aperçu general sur l'Egypte*. Paris: Fortin, Masson, 1840 (2 vols.).

Hamont, P.N. *L'Egypte sous Méhémet Ali*. Paris: Leautey et Lecointe, 1843 (2 vols.).

Al-Jabarti, 'Abd al-Rahman. *'Aja'ib al-Athar fi'l-Tarajim wa'l-Akhbar*. Ed. and trans. Thomas Philipp and Moshe Perlmann. Stuttgart: Steiner, 1994 (4 vols.).

Lindsay, A.W.C. *Letters on Egypt, Edom, and the Holy Land*. London: Henry Colborn, 1838 (2 vols.).

Madden, Richard. *Egypt and Mohammed Ali*. London: Hamilton, 1841.

Measor, H.P. *A Tour in Egypt, Arabia Petræa and the Holy Land in the Years 1841–2*. London: Rivington, 1844.

Paton, A.A. *History of the Egyptian Revolution*. London: Trubner, 1863 (2 vols.).

Pückler-Muskau (Prince). *Egypt under Mehemet Ali*. Trans. H. Evans Lloyd. London: H. Colburn, 1845 (2 vols.).

Sami, Amin. *Taqwim al-Nil.* Cairo: Dar al-Kutub, 1928 (3 vols.).

St. John, J. A. *Egypt and Mohammed Ali.* London: Longman, 1834 (2 vols.).

Scott, C.R. *Rambles in Egypt and Candia.* London: Henry Colborn, 1837 (2 vols.).

Waghorn, Thomas. *Egypt in 1837.* London: Smith Elder, 1837.

Al-Waqa'i' al-Misriyya, issue no. 3, 29 Jumad al-Thani 1244/6 January 1829.

Wilde, W.R. *Narrative of a Voyage in … Algiers, Egypt, Palestine, etc.* Dublin: William Curry, 1844.

Wilkinson, J.G. *Modern Egypt and Thebes.* London: John Murray, 1843.

MODERN SCHOLARSHIP

'Abd al-Karim, Ahmed I. *Tarikh al-Ta'lim fi 'Asr Muhammad 'Ali (History of Education in the Reign of Mehmed Ali).* Cairo: al-Nahda al-Misriyya, 1938.

Abdel-Nasser, Gamal. *al-Mithaq (The Charter).* Cairo: Dar al-Ta'awun, 1962.

'Abduh, Muhammad. "Athar Muhammad 'Ali fi Misr." *Al-Manar,* v. 5, pt. 5, 7 June 1902, 179.

Antonius, George. *The Arab Awakening: The Story of the Arab National Movement.* London: Hamish Hamilton, 1938.

Baer, Gabriel. *A History of Landownership in Modern Egypt, 1800–1950.* Oxford: Oxford University Press, 1962.

Barakat, 'Ali. *Tatawwur al-Milkiyya al-Zira'iyya fi Misr wa Atharuhu 'ala al-Haraka al-Siyasiyya (Development of Landownership in Egypt and its Impact on the Political Movement).* Cairo: Dar al-Thaqada al-Jadida, 1977.

Bartle, G. F. "Bowring and the Near Eastern crisis of 1838–1840." *The English Historical Review,* v. 79, 1964, 761–774.

Cuno, Kenneth. *The Pasha's Peasants: Land, Society, and Economy in Lower Egypt, 1740–1858.* Cambridge: Cambridge University Press, 1992.

———. "Muhammad Ali and the decline and revival thesis in modern Egyptian history." In Raouf Abbas, Ed. *Islah am Tahdith? Misr fi 'Ahd Muhammad Ali (Reform or Modernization? Egypt in the Reign of Mehmed Ali).* Cairo: al-Majlis al-A'la lil-Thaqafa, 2000, 93–119.

———. "Constructing Muhammad Ali," *al-Ahram Weekly,* 10–17 November 2005.

Di Capua, Yoav. "The thought and practice of modern Egyptian historiography, 1890–1970." PhD dissertation, Princeton University, 2004.

Dodwell, Henry. *The Founder of Modern Egypt: A Study of Muhammad 'Ali.* Cambridge: Cambridge University Press, 1931.

Douin, Georges, ed. *La Mission du Baron de Boislecomte, L'Egypte et la Syrie en 1833.* Cairo: Royal Egyptian Geographical Society, 1927.

Fahmy, Khaled. *All the Pasha's Men: Mehmed Ali, His Army and the Making of Modern Egypt.* Cambridge: Cambridge University Press, 1997.

———. "Medicine and power: towards a social history of medicine in nineteenth-century Egypt." *Cairo Papers in the Social Sciences,* v. 23, 2000, 1–45.

———. "Women, medicine and power in nineteenth-century Egypt." In Lila Abu Lughod, ed. *Remaking Women: Feminism and Modernity in the Middle East.* Princeton: Princeton University Press, 1998, 35–72.

Fahmy, Mustafa. *La Révolution de l'industrie en Égypte et ses consequences sociales au 19e siècle (1800–1850).* Leiden: Brill, 1954.

Ghazaleh, Pascale. "Masters of the trade: crafts and craftspeople in Cairo, 1750–1850." *Cairo Papers in Social Sciences,* v. 22, 1999.

Ghorbal, Shafik. *The Beginnings of the Egyptian Question and the Rise of Mehemet Ali.* London: Routledge, 1928.

———. *Muhammad 'Ali al-Kabir (Mehmed Ali the Great).* Cairo: Da'irat al-Ma'arif al-Islamiyya, 1944.

Heyworth-Dunne, J. *An Introduction to the History of Education in Modern Egypt.* London: Frank Cass, 1938.

Al-Hitta, Ahmed. *Tarikh al-Zira'a al-Misriyya fi 'Ahd Muhammad 'Ali al-Kabir (History of Egyptian Agriculture in the Reign of Mehmed Ali the Great).* Cairo: Dar al-Ma'arif, 1936.

Hunter, F. Robert. *Egypt Under the Khedives, 1805–1879: From Household Government to Modern Bureaucracy.* Pittsburgh: University of Pittsburgh Press, 1984.

Al-Jiritli, 'Ali. *Tarikh al-Sina'a fi Misr fi al-Nisf al-Awwal min al-Qarn al-Tasi' 'Ashr (History of Industry in Egypt in the First Half of the Nineteenth Century).* Cairo: Dar al-Ma'arif, 1952.

Kuhnke, Laverne. *Lives at Risk: Public Health in Nineteenth-Century Egypt.* Berkeley: University of California Press, 1990.

Kutluoğlu, Muhammed. *The Egyptian Question (1831–1841).* Istanbul: Eren, 1998.

Murray, Charles A. *A Short Memoir of Mohammed Ali.* London: Quaritch, 1898.

Nallino, Maria. "Some notes on two Arabic translations of Machiavelli's *The Prince.*" In *al-Ishamat al-Italiyya fi Dirasat Misr al-Haditha fi 'Asr Muhammad Ali (Italian Contribution to the Study of Modern Egypt in the Reign of Mehmed Ali).* Cairo: al-Majlis al-A'la lil-Thaqafa, 2005.

Owen, E.R.J. *Cotton and the Egyptian Economy, 1820–1914: A Study in Trade and Development.* Oxford: Clarendon Press, 1969.

———. *The Middle East in the World Economy, 1800–1914.* London: Methuen, 1981.

Peters, Rudolph. *Crime and Punishment in Islamic Law.* Cambridge: Cambridge University Press, 2005.

Radwan, Abul-Futuh. *Tarikh Matba'at Bulaq (The History of the Bulaq Press).* Cairo: al-Matba'ah al-'Amiriyyah, 1953.

Al-Rafi'i, 'Abd al-Rahman. *'Asr Muhammad Ali (Mehmed Ali's Reign).* Cairo: n.p., 1930.

Rivlin, Helen. *The Agricultural Policy of Muhammad Ali in Egypt.* Cambridge, Mass.: Harvard University Press, 1961.

Al-Sayyid Marsot, Afaf L. *Egypt in the Reign of Muhammad Ali.* Cambridge: Cambridge University Press, 1984.

Sonbol, Amira. *The Creation of a Medical Profession in Egypt, 1800–1922.* Syracuse: Syracuse University Press, 1991.

Temperley, H.W.V. *England and the Near East: The Crimea.* London: Longman, 1964.

Tucker, Judith. *Women in Nineteenth-Century Egypt.* Cambridge: Cambridge University Press, 1985.

Tugay, Emine F. *Three Centuries: Family Chronicles of Turkey and Egypt.* London: Oxford University Press, 1963.

INDEX